HERALDIC SYMBOLS

HERALDIC SYMBOLS

ISLAMIC INSIGNIA AND WESTERN HERALDRY

William Leaf · Sally Purcell

VICTORIA AND ALBERT MUSEUM

Published by the Victoria and Albert Museum, London 1986
Text © 1986 Trustees of the Victoria and Albert Museum
Illustrations © 1986 Trustees of the Victoria and Albert Museum or as acknowledged
All rights reserved

ISBN 0 905209 92 3

Designed by Tim Harvey
Produced by the South Leigh Press Ltd, The Studio, Chilcroft Road, Kingsley Green,
Haslemere, Surrey
Phototypeset by AKM Associates (UK) Ltd, Ajmal House, Hayes Road, Southall, London
Printed in Great Britain by R.J. Acford Ltd, Chichester, Sussex

Frontispiece: A stained glass roundle with a
border of merchants' marks.

CONTENTS

FOREWORD

By definition a Museum is a shrine of the Muses; and in this context Clio is not the least important. Heraldry has been called the shorthand of history. Happily the Victoria and Albert Museum has always been rich in examples of armorial art; for it is one of the characteristics of heraldry that it can lend its colour or its romance to virtually any form of applied art. This book is not merely a catalogue of the numerous manifestations of blazon in this great collection. The authors bring two special slants to such an exercise. Sally Purcell has used her wide knowledge of mediaeval French and Provençal to illumine the development of heraldry, as seen through the attitudes of those who created the great romantic poems and assisted in breaking the grip of Latin upon literature in the Middle Ages. William Leaf has employed his considerable studies of Islamic heraldry and artefacts to extend the scope of the text and remind us that the need for identification transgressed the boundaries between the Muslim world and crusading Christendom. So also the capacities of heraldry for decorative use outlasted its original employment in battlefield or tournament and have carried themselves with vigour and variety into the twentieth century. Some of the objects illustrated have been familiar to me for well over sixty years; it is my hope that *Heraldic Symbols* will bring their beauty and their storied background to an ever wider audience.

Michael Maclagan FSA
Richmond Herald
and Emeritus Fellow of Trinity College, Oxford

INTRODUCTION

The meaning of Heraldry

To understand best the meaning of the word Heraldry — or Armory as it was called before the Heralds came to have almost a monopoly over its administration[1] — I think one should take notice of one of the greatest modern scholars on the subject. Sir Anthony Wagner, until quite recently Garter King of Arms and now Clarenceux, in *Heralds and Heraldry in the Middle Ages* (1939, 2nd ed. 1956), wrote as follows: 'True heraldry I would define as the systematic use of hereditary devices centred on the shield'.

These two points, the principle of heredity and the importance of the shield, must be kept firmly in mind. However, it should not be imagined that the science of Heraldry sprang fully armed like Athene from the head of Zeus.

Late mediaeval writers on the subject certainly speculated that coat armour was first worn in heaven and that the heavenly host was arrayed like some baronial levée beneath its banners. Lady Juliana Berners, whose *Boke of St. Albans*, first printed in 1486, relies heavily on Nicholas Upton's *De Studio Militari* (written a generation earlier, in 1446–7), was firmly of this opinion. Gerard Legh in his *Accedens of Armory*, first published in 1562, gives a list of the arms of the Nine Worthies, Duke Joshua, Hector, David, Alexander, Judas Macchabeus, Charlemagne, Julius Caesar, King Arthur and Sir Guy Earl of Warwicke. Approximately thirty years later Shakespeare, in Act V Scene 2 of *Loves Labours Lost*, makes fun of these gentlemen and their arms, for the rustic schoolmaster Holofernes is forced from the stage by the cruel sarcasm of the courtiers when he tries to put on a pageant of the Worthies.

The *Blazon of Gentrie* by Sir John Ferne, published in 1586, ascribes arms to such as Adam, Jabal and Jubal, Naamah and Tubal Cain. The immensely popular *A Display of Heraldrie*, by John Guillim, Rouge Croix Pursuivant, of which the first seven editions came out in 1611, repeats many of the former fantasies, but also sounds a note of warning: 'The antiquity of the gentilical arms in Britain will prove of far later date than many of our gentry would willingly be thought to have borne them.'

Pre-Heraldry in the ancient world

In prehistoric times many tribes were totemistic and treated certain animals or birds as their sacred protectors. In *The Golden Fleece*, Professor Robert Graves describes some of the heroes who have answered the call of Jason's 'herald' to join the *Argo*: Mopsos had a starling crest, and the tip of his tongue was slit with a knife. Castor and Polydeuces, sons of Leda by Almighty Zeus, were adorned with swans' feather headdresses and cloaks of

swansdown. Gloomy Melampos of Argos, a cousin of Jason, wore the magpie crest, and hot-tempered Eriginos of Miletos a cloak striped like a tunny-fish and a belt of plaited horse-hair, *in honour of his father Poseidon.*

The contest between Athene and Poseidon for the land of Attica is well known: in the Erechtheum the goddess produced the olive, her symbol, and the god the salt spring and the horse. Athene was chosen as the titular deity, and another of her attributes, the sacred owl, still appears on the Greek coins.

During the long centuries when the Pharaohs ruled the valley of the Nile and exerted their influence north into the countries of the Eastern Mediterranean, symbols of divinity and kingship were formulated. At the battle of Kadesh, fought by the young Raamses II against the Hittites in 1296 BC, we know that he commanded four bodies of troops named after the gods Re, Amun, Ptah and Setekh; each of these marched under distinctive insignia – the earthly image of the four gods who, in this campaign, were the protectors of the Living Horus, the Pharaoh Raamses.

In Mesopotamia, where Sumerians, Babylonians, Assyrians and Hittites fought and made treaties, pillaged and traded, incised seals were used to sign

Fig.2 The impressions of four cylinder seals:
a] Mushesh-Ninurta (*c.* 850 BC)
b] a mounted warrior beneath astral symbols
c] a religious figure flanked by winged bulls
d] the Achaemenid king Darius I (*re.* 512–486 BC).
Courtesy of the British Museum

a

b

c

d

their edicts and to identify and protect their merchandise and other belongings. The cylinder seal often combined attributes of the gods with more personal emblems and so, as the pattern could be reproduced indefinitely, even large objects which bore its impression would be assured of the absolute protection of the god.

The Persian Achaemenid dynasty (558–330 BC), though professedly dualistic by religion, inherited the many and varied symbols – monstrous, astronomical and naturalistic – of previous theogonies, and it was in this period that we can find the beginnings of tribal and family insignia.

Alexander of Macedonia, when he conquered this vast Empire, took to himself many of the divine attributes of his predecessors, and his Seleucid and Diodotid successors in Asia followed his example. The Hellenistic Bactrians and the Parthian Arsacids formed trading and cultural connections

Fig.3 Silver plate of the Sassanian king Peroz
(*re.* AD 459–484), armed and crowned, hunting
boars. *Courtesy of the Freer Gallery of Art,
Smithsonian Institution, Washington DC*

with the Chinese, and these links seem to have continued into Sassanid times
(AD 226–641). In the *Shahnamah* (*Book of the Rulers* — of Iran), completed by
Abu'l Kasim Firdausi on 25 February 1010, 'the Khan called to him three
hundred of his servants, each of whom carried a banner according to the
Chinese fashion, and a standard of shining Chinese brocade was raised
beneath which the brightness of the sun disappeared'. The royal standard
was said to be a workman's apron covered with brocade from Byzantium,
and decorated with a figure of jewel-stones on a gold background; it was
surmounted by a golden ball in the shape of the moon. From it floated

streamers of red, yellow and violet material; it was called the *Kaweiani direfesch* (the standard of Kawa), and each successive ruler added new jewels and rich brocades to the ignoble blacksmith's apron. 'Thus the standard of Kawa shone in the night like the sun and gave new hope to everyone who saw it . . . When it flew in the midst of an encampment of tents white, sable, violet and blue, Kawa's standard made the world look yellow, red and violet'. When it was captured at the battle of Kadisiya in 637 it measured 24 by 15 feet, and was sold for 30,000 dinars, though it was believed to be worth over a million.

Individual warriors are mentioned as having their own devices – eagles, boars, dragons, moons and suns – some of which, we are told, were handed on to their sons; we know from surviving reliefs that Sassanian nobles surrounding the king also had distinctive devices which they bore on their bonnets of rank. These are not unlike the tribal signs which are found throughout the Near and Middle East from a very early date, and which are used alongside more conventional charges in the twelfth century, when insignia reappear in Syria and Egypt under the Ayyubid and later the Mamluk sultans (see below, *tamgas*).

In the West too there is evidence that tribal and military emblems were used. Tacitus and Plutarch mention animals on the shields of Celtic and Germanic tribesmen respectively, and it is possible that the designs found on Gaulish, Pictish and early Scottish inscribed stones have some totemistic significance.

However, it can safely be said that nothing we have noticed so far can be construed as true Heraldry, as defined by Sir Anthony Wagner, whose view, I feel, all sensible heraldists must follow.

The motifs of Heraldry were there — direct and easily recognisable objects which said in effect: 'this is who I am' or 'this is my lord'; 'this belongs to me' or 'this is under the protection of such-a-one'. Astrological signs, the composite beasts of Gizeh, Nineveh and Susa, the whorls and geometrical shapes of Celtic art, the animals and birds of Greek coins, of Roman ensigns, or of the banners of Iranian nobles — all these, and many more, would become the *charges* (see Glossary) of Heraldry, but it took a massing of military forces from the West and the East to supply the necessary impetus.

This impetus was provided at the end of the eleventh century by what were called the Holy Wars, now generally named the Crusades.

CHAPTER I

HERALDIC GRAMMAR

Before looking at the developments which took place in the Middle East and in Western Europe during the twelfth and thirteenth centuries, it would be as well to concentrate first on the language, or grammar, of Heraldry. Contrary to popular belief, this is logical, easy to understand and easy to use. The terms are mostly Norman French, which was then the language of the ruling class, though they have often been anglicized.

The most important part of the *full achievement* or *coat of arms* is the *shield* (which is surmounted by a *helm* encircled by a *torse* [wreath] and bearing in most cases a *crest*) framed by the *lambrequin* (mantling) issuing from the wreath and held up, where appropriate, by *supporters* standing on a *compartment*, often strewn with *badges*.

The Tinctures

When describing a shield (which can be of various shapes, realistic until about 1500, in later times often fantastic) the background, or *field*, is named first. This can be of metal: either *or*, gold, from Latin *aureus*; or *argent*, silver, from Latin *argenteus* (normally rendered as yellow and white, for reasons of cost in the case of gold and because of the fear of oxidation in the case of silver); or one of five colours: *gules*, *gueules*, *gowles*, red, from Old French *gole*, *geule*, 'an animal's mouth or throat'; *azur*, azure, an Old French word meaning blue, derived from Arabic *azul*; *sable*, black, from the colour of the fur of that animal; *vert* (pronounced *verte* so that it cannot be confused with *vair* – see below), from Latin *viridis*, from which we get the word *viridian*; and more unusually *purpure*, purple, Low Latin *porporius*, from Greek *porphuros*; or of a fur. The furs most in use are *ermine*, formalised black tails on a white ground, and its reverse *ermines*; *erminois*, black tails on a gold ground, and its reverse *pean*; and *vair*, which is composed of alternate blue and white bell-shaped skins which are supposed to represent the backs and stomachs of blue-grey squirrels. In mediaeval romances heroes and heroines are often described as having eyes of *vair*, and Cinderella wore at the ball *vair* (not *verre*, glass) slippers! If the panels are coloured, for example, gold and red, then the field is described as *vairé, vairy of or and gules* (Ferrers).

If a charge is painted in its natural colours it is blasoned as *proper*; Cambridge or RAF blue is called *bleu céleste* or *sky blue*; and skin-colour is called *carnation* (from Latin *caro, carnis*, flesh). The stains are *tenné* (Old French *tané*, tanned, probably from Celtic Breton *tann*, oak), orange-tawny; *murrey*, mulberry-coloured, from Latin *morum*; and *sanguine*, blood-red, from Latin *sanguineus*. Only sky-blue, as far as I know, is used as a field colour, and the three stains are rarely used for anything other than livery colours.

a

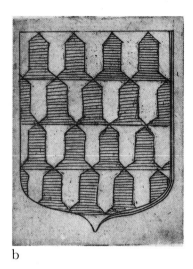

b

c

In early literary sources, such as the *Chansons de geste*, other colours are mentioned. We find *escus* (pointed escutcheons) and *targes* (round bucklers usually associated with Saracens, though they also used pointed shields) that are *blanc* (white), *vermeil* (crimson), *bloi(s)* (bruise-coloured), *bis* (greyish-brown), *porprin* (purple), and most confusingly *sinople* (red),[2] which some time during the late fourteenth or early fifteenth century came to mean green – and is still so used in heraldic French, Spanish and Dutch (with the alternative *groen* in Dutch).

As I mentioned above, it would seem an obvious expedient not to use two homonyms, *vert* and *vair*. I have, in fact, a painted armorial of the Sherbrooke family where the field is coloured green, though the correct *blazon* (description)[3] should be *vair, a chief or, over all on a bend gules three pierced mullets argent.* However, it seems ludicrous to imagine a logical French herald or king at arms sitting down to consider the problem, summoning his assistant or pursuivant and saying like Archimedes, 'Eureka! We'll use sinople for green' – forgetting that for close on three hundred years it had meant red.

When a coat of arms is not coloured the tinctures can be indicated in one of two ways; the first is hatching, using a system originated by Silvestro di Petra Sancta, S.J., from whose *Tesserae gentilitiae* (1638) the majority of hatched examples in this book are taken. *Or* is represented by dots, *argent* by a plain surface, *gules* by vertical lines, *azure* by horizontal lines, *sable* by horizontal and vertical lines, *vert* by diagonals from *dexter chief* (that is, the right-hand top corner if you are behind the shield) to *sinister base*, and *purpure*

AD REM.

Pl.II Rasulid perfume sprinkler.

Fig.5 Arms of the Bavarian family of von Sandizell in stained glass: *Or, a buffalo's head sable langued gules and horned argent*. The diapering breaks up the field effectively without detracting from the importance of the charge.

by the reverse of *vert*. Alternatively, the field and charges can be *tricked*, that is, the appropriate abbreviation is written in the correct area of the blazon: or, o.; arg., ar.; gu., g.; az., b. (for blue); sa., s.; ver., v.; purp., p.

Plain (or *uncharged*) shields, except for those that are *vairé*, are comparatively rare, though Woodward in his admirable *Treatise on Heraldry British and Foreign*, published in 1892, writes: 'I venture to affirm that there is no subject on which so many books have been published with so little research as Heraldry; and I may be allowed to express a hope that the list above given [of plain shields] which will hardly escape the hands of future freebooting "compilers", may be useful as saving them from writing nonsense as to coats of a single metal or colour being "almost unknown". If to the forty, or thereby, coats of plain metal or colour given above there be added the many coats in which a single fur is the sole charge, there will be I dare say at least a hundred examples of a use, which is certainly curious and infrequent, but which is not of such extreme rarity as is often ignorantly asserted.'

Plain shields and large uncharged areas of more complicated shields, either of field or charge, were often decorated. This decoration is called *diapering* (Old French *diaspre* from Med.Lat. *diasprum*, 'a patterned cloth', original Latin *jaspis*, 'the jewelstone jasper'). It consists of arabesques, floral designs, or any other pattern which seems artistically appropriate. The design is often of a different tint from the background; black, gold, or silver are also used, and care must be taken that it is not so forcefully executed as to give the impression of a number of small charges (see below, *semy*).

Honourable Ordinaries

To Mr Woodward I will return again soon, but for the moment let us go back to the arms of Sherbrooke already mentioned and examine the blazon more closely: the field is *vair*, there is a *chief* of gold, and over both these is a red bend charged with three silver *pierced mullets*, or *molets*. The *chief* is the top, or head, part of the shield (Old French *chef*, head) and also heads the list of geometrical divisions which are called *honourable ordinaries*, and are mentioned immediately after the field. Second to the *chief* comes the *cross*, of which there are many variations, including the *saltire* or *St. Andrew's Cross*, which by some authorities is considered a separate ordinary. Again contrary to popular belief, the cross on a family's coat of arms does *not* mean that the founder of the line was necessarily a crusader. Thirdly comes the *fesse*, called a *bar* if it is reduced in width, which runs horizontally across the centre of the shield; a vertical band is called a *pale*, often reduced to a *palet*; a *bend*, or *bend sinister*, is a diagonal band, the first starting from dexter chief, the second

Fig.6 From Petra Sancta: chief, cross and saltire:

a] *Argent, a chief gules* – marquises of Montferrat, Piedmont

b] *Argent, a cross azure* – Guthrie of that Ilk, Scotland

c] *Gules, a cross engrailed or* – Bouchavesnes, Artois

d] *Or, a saltire and a chief gules* – Bruce of Annandale, Scotland.

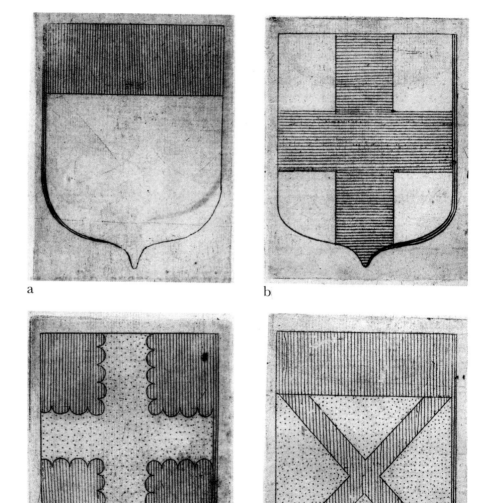

a

b

c

d

Fig.7 From Petra Sancta: fesse, palets and bends:
a] *Vert, a fesse argent* – Inpruck, Austria
b] *Gules, 3 palets argent, a Latin cross of the 1st in the dexter palet of the 2nd* – Grimani, Venice
c] *Sable, a bend or* – Galler von Schwarzenegg, Austria
d] *Azure, 3 bendlets sinister chequy argent and gules* – Groschlag von Diepurg, Palatinate of the Rhine.

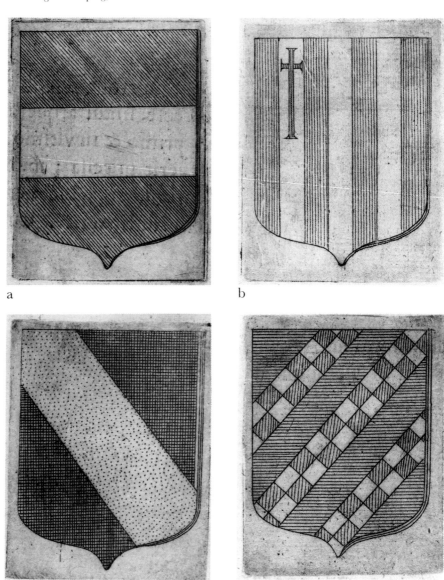

a   b

c   d

Fig.8 From Petra Sancta: the Royal Arms of Scotland.

from sinister chief, and traversing the entire field. When reduced it is known as a *bendlet*; a *bendlet couped* (cut) at either end is called a *baton* or *baston*. A *baton sinister* (not a *bar* sinister, which is an obvious nonsense),[4] is frequently used to denote royal bastardy. Another way to denote bastardy is to surround the arms with a *bordure*, sometimes plain, but more often *compony*, i.e., made with bricks of alternate tincture and metal. A bordure runs around the entire field; if it is thinner and leaves a space at its outermost edge it is called an *orle*; an *orle voided*, that is, with its centre cut out, is called a *double tressure*. This is much used in Scottish heraldry, for the royal arms are *or, a lion rampant within a double tressure flory counter-flory gules*. An inverted V is called a *chevron*, and when reduced in width a *chevronel*.

These diminutives, as J. Brooke-Little (then Richmond Herald, now Norroy and Ulster King of Arms) says in *An Heraldic Alphabet*, '. . . were not used in early blazon . . . The bar and the baton are the only two . . . which have a decent antiquity. It is a hopeful sign that these niceties of blazon . . . are now seldom used by the kings of arms.'

Perhaps the most satisfactory theory of the origin of these honourable ordinaries is that they represent bands of wood strengthening the *cuir bouillé* shield, as in the Bayeux Tapestry. In early literature, *bande* was used much more freely than in later times, to denote a number of geometrical additions to the field.

The field itself can be divided *per fesse*, *per pale*, *per bend* (or *per bend sinister*),

Fig.9 From Petra Sancta: inescutcheons, bordures and chevronels:

a] *Argent, an inescutcheon gules within an orle of papegays vert, legged, beaked and collared of the 2nd –* Bournel, Forez

b] *Argent, a bordure engrailed per pale or and azure –* Popoleschi, Florence

c] *Per pale argent and sable, a chevron countercharged* – Renier, Venice

d] *Argent, 3 chevronels gules* – du Plessis Richelieu.

a

b

c

d

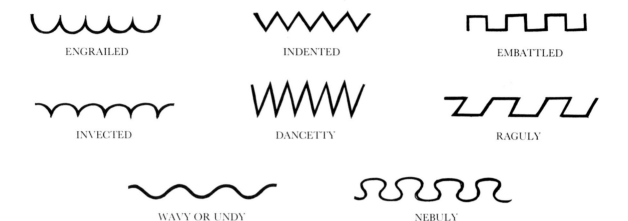

Fig.10 Examples of lines of division.

ENGRAILED   INDENTED   EMBATTLED

INVECTED   DANCETTY   RAGULY

WAVY OR UNDY   NEBULY

per chevron, or by multiple lines such as *barry, paly, bendy*, or *chevronny* of the number of divisions: these lines can be of various patterns, of which the commonest are given here. The lines of division can cross each other to form a number of attractive fields. Thus lines, for example, *paly* and *barry* form *chequy*, a chessboard pattern, which is often given to Saracen warriors both in the *Chansons de geste* and in later Romances. An interesting description of a horse trapper is given by Richard the Pilgrim (*c.* 1150) in his *Chanson de Jérusalem*, which was worked over by Graindor de Douai in the early thirteenth century:

> d'un vermeil siglaton ovré a eschequier
> fu covers li chevaux: menu l'ot fait trenchier
> le blanc par mi le roge véissiés blanchoier

> Of crimson silk worked into chessboard squares
> this trapper was: and through the holes cut there
> the horse's milk-white coat showed clear.

In two fifteenth-century manuscripts of the arms of the knights of the Round Table, to the paynim Palamedes is attributed *eschequettes d'argent et de sable*, to his kinsmen Saphar, *party per pale, vair and checky or and vert*, and to Esclabor, *checky or and gules*. Saracens certainly did have these geometrically divided blazons.

Dr Juan Zozaya Stabel-Hansen has provided me with these two quotations from the *Annales Palatinos de Al-Hakam II* for the year 971: Hisam leaves al-Zahra '. . . preceded by different classes of banners and ensigns, among which, for the special honour with which his lord distinguished him,

23

was the lofty Satrany (Checkerboard)', and on 25 November, Galib ibn Abd
al-Rahman sends a military detachment to the Alcazar of Córdoba '. . . in
perfect formation, with parade ornaments including the Satrany'. In the
Department of Ceramics at the Victoria and Albert Museum is a small black
perfume sprinkler, inscribed *Abu l'Fath Umar ibn Sultan Al-Malik Muzaffar*
(that is, the Rasulid sultan of Yaman al-Ashraf Abu l'Fath Umar who
reigned from July 1295 to November 1296) and decorated with red and
white flowers and roundles *argent, four bars of wedges alternately gules and sable*,
insignia which were used by other Rasulids (see Plate II).

Fig.12 From Petra Sancta: chequy, quarterly
and gyronny:
a] *Chequy or and azure* – Dreux, France
b] *Quarterly, or and gules* – Mandeville, earls of
Essex
c] *Gyronny of 12 gules and or* – Bassingbourne,
Essex

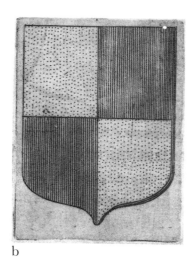

a   b   c

The Sub-Ordinaries

The more important sub-ordinaries are the *canton*, which takes up one eighth of the shield, the *quarter*, both usually placed in dexter chief, and the *gyron*, which is half a quarter per bend. Many families bear *quarterly* or *gyronny* arms, such as Mandeville, Earls of Essex, *quarterly or and gules*, and a number of related houses, who differenced this coat, e.g., de Vere, Earls of Oxford, *quarterly gules and or, in the first quarter a molet argent*. The basic arms of the clan Campbell are *gyronny or and sable* of various numbers, which are differenced in many ways (see below).

The *fret* is quite commonly used, and a field may be *fretty*, that is, covered with bendlets and bendlets sinister woven over and under, and sometimes nailed. The arms of Maltravers, *sable, a fret or*, provide a good example of *canting*, or punning, for it's obviously 'hard to get through' a piece of trellis.

The *inescutcheon* is a small shield placed in the middle of the field, and if it is *voided* it can easily be confused with an *orle*. The inescutcheon plays a very important part in Heraldry, for the arms of an heraldic heiress (not necessarily the inheritrix of a property: three sisters who have no brother are all co-heiresses of their father's arms) are placed in this way upon her husband's arms, as an *inescutcheon of pretence*. The children of this marriage will then quarter their parental arms, and as long as that family exists these arms would remain quartered. If other heiresses later married into the family, their arms too would be added, and the ridiculous state of a shield with a hundred quarterings could arise!

Fig.13 After Petra Sancta: the Maltravers fret
(*sable, fretty or*)

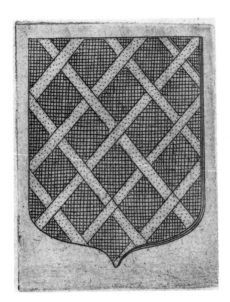

As we have seen, the purpose of the armorial shield and the banner was to provide sure and instant identification in the heat of battle. The seal did the same job in peace-time: it said in effect, 'these are the baron's arms, this is his possession'. If the baron married an heiress and partook of part or the whole of her property, it was necessary to relay this information to an illiterate society: 'the baron now claims feudal rights over his own and his wife's property'.

It now appears obvious that quartering is the way to express this fact, but other ways were tried and discarded for practical reasons. Of these, the grouping of shields and *dimidiation* are the best known. In the latter, the two shields are cut in half and placed next to each other, the husband's (but in some cases the dominant partner's) on the dexter, the wife's on the sinister. The system of dimidiation produced some rather extraordinary arms, such as lions with fishes' tails (Great Yarmouth), but, more importantly, led to confusion where *chevronny* must be blazoned as *bendy*.

Instances may be found where a stone-carver has correctly placed the arms of an heiress *in pretence* in the centre (or *fesse point*), but has wrongly also *impaled* the lady's arms. Like *dimidiation*, *impalement* is the placing of two coats of arms side by side, but here there is no confusion as to blazoning, as the entire arms are shown (except in the case of a *bordure*, an *orle*, or a *tressure*, for these charges are not normally continued down the palar line).

Impalement records an alliance between two families for the duration of a marriage only, and the offspring do not inherit their mother's arms.

Fig.14 Hispano-Moresque tile with the arms of Castile (*gules, a tower triple-towered or*) and León (*argent, a lion rampant purpure*) quarterly. This quartered coat is one of the earliest and signifies the unification of the two kingdoms under Ferdinand the Saint in 1229. His daughter Eleanor married Edward I of England and these arms appear on her tomb in Westminster Abbey.

A *lozenge* is a diamond shape; when it is voided it is known as a *mascle*, and one that is elongated, but not voided, is a *fusil*. These three charges are seldom borne singly: lozenges, mascles and fusils often appear *in fesse*, or in patterns of three or more rows.

Hatchments

The lozenge forms the cartouche for the arms of an unmarried lady or a widow, and for the display of funereal arms. In many churches throughout the British Isles can be found large lozenge-shaped boards on which are represented the arms of local families. These are usually very accurately

Fig.15 Chinese export porcelain:
1 and 4: *argent, 3 martlets between 2 chevronels gules* (*recte* tinctures reversed) – Peach
2 and 3: *sable, on a bend argent 3 roses gules, in chief a chessrook of 2nd* – Small als Smalley
On an inescutcheon and accollé: *argent, 3 cocks gules* – Cockburn.

Fig.16 From Petra Sancta: lozenges, mascles and fusils:
a] *Gules, 4 lozenges in fesse argent* – d'Aubigny als d'Albini, earls of Bridgewater
b] *Azure, 10 mascles 3,3,3 and 1 or* (*recte, on a canton a lion passant guardant or*) – Bruges, earls of Winchester
c] *Argent, 3 fusils in fesse gules* – Montacute, earls of Salisbury.

a

b

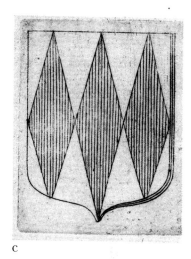

c

represented, considering that they were done by the estate coach-painter or a local sign-writer; the majority are painted on either wood or stretched canvas, though framed examples in other media do occur.

They are called *hatchments*, a name derived from 'achievement', and are used to commemorate the death of an armigerous local squire or nobleman. The custom originated in the Low Countries and was adopted here in the early seventeenth century, at which time the boards were usually rectangular and much smaller. They were placed over the front door of the house where the dead person had lived, carried in the funeral cortège, and then laid up either on the wall of a private chapel or in the body of the church.

The background behind the arms of the dead person was painted black, so if a wife predeceased her husband the dexter side would be white and the sinister black; when the husband died the old board could be taken down and more black paint added, or a new one could be designed. Mr Peter Summers, the editor of *Hatchments in Britain*, has suggested that the practice of both impaling and placing on an inescutcheon the arms of an heiress arose because it would be impossible to show the death of an heiress if her arms occupied only the centre of her husband's shield. Below the arms, in place of the family's motto, is usually written a pious tag such as *RESURGAM* (I shall rise again), *IN COELO QUIES* (In heaven there is rest), or *MORS JANUA VITAE* (Death is the gate to life). When a Bishop or the head of a College dies, the hatchment shows his personal arms impaling those of the See or College, as if he were its wife; the background behind that part of the shield should always be white, as the office never dies.

Fig.17 Hatchment from All Saints, Hastings, of
Lillies Macmillan (*b.* 1752–*d.*1801) first wife of
John Scott, merchant of Hastings, who
differences the arms of Scott with *a bordure
engrailed gules.* A pious tag is more commonly
used than the family motto. *Photo J.Bone*

Fig.18 Royal arms as used by the House of
Stuart, dated the year of the Restoration of
Charles II.

Fig.19 Cadency marks.

Pl.III Glass dish with the arms of Louis XII (re.1498–1515): France modern (*azure, 3 fleurs-de-lys or*) dimidiated with those of Anne, duchess of Brittany (*d.1514*) (*argent, 3 rows of ermine tails*, i.e. *ermine plain*). This is an extremely late example of dimidiation and it is curious that only the French arms are treated in this way.

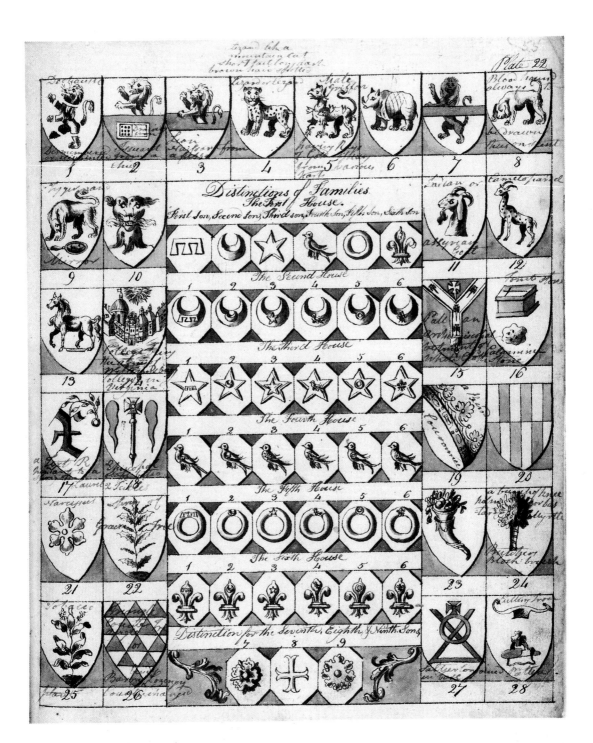

Pl.IV Hatchment of Elizabeth duchess of Buccleuch (*d.* 21 November 1827), widow of Henry the 3rd duke (*d.* 11 January 1812). Her arms – quarterly Montagu and Monthermer – appear in the second grand quarter and upon an inescutcheon. The first grand quarter has the arms of Charles II *debruised by a baton sinister argent*; the third has Douglas and Mar quarterly, the fourth Scott. The dexter supporter is the unicorn of Scotland, the sinister *a griffin or, winged, beaked and membered sable* for Montagu. *Courtesy of Peter Summers, photo J. Bone.*

Fig.20 From Petra Sancta: billets and bezants:
a] *Or, 3 billets gules* – van Franckenberg-en-
Prochlitz, Holland
b] *Or, billety gules* – St. Martin, Normandy
c] *Sable, 14 bezants 4,4,3 and 3* – Suriche, Liège

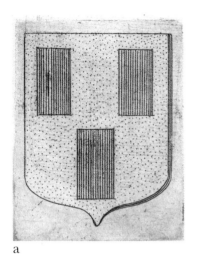
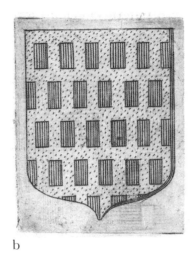
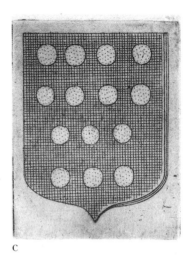

a   b   c

This practice has been virtually discontinued, though Mr Summers has noted eighty dating from this century. Although, like carved ledger stones and other church monuments, they can be misleading, it is often possible to learn a great deal about the history of a family by studying a series of hatchments in conjunction with other records.

Also in many Anglican churches one will find a board or metal plaque (occasionally a wall painting) of the Royal Arms. This is to show the force of the Act of Supremacy of 1534, which appointed Henry VIII and his successors 'Proctector and Only Supreme Head of the Church and Clergy of England'. Close study of these will show how the arms have changed from that time to the present – the arms of Ireland were added in the third quarter; Scotland has been settled since 1714 in the second; France was moved around and eventually abandoned in 1801. The arms of Nassau were borne in pretence by William III, and those of Hanover in the fourth quarter by George I and II and in pretence by Geroge III and IV and William IV, until they too were lost, as Victoria could not inherit that kingdom. Since her accession in 1837 the arms have remained: Quarterly 1 & 4 England: *gules, three lions passant guardant or*; 2 Scotland: *or, a lion rampant within a double tressure flory counter-flory gules;* 3 Ireland: *azure, a harp or stringed argent.*

Arms of younger sons

A *label* is not usually borne as a charge, but it is important as it is used for denoting the arms of an eldest son during the lifetime of his father. In England and Ireland, since the early sixteenth century, specific charges

Fig.21 From Petra Sancta: crusilly, floretty and a bend of France:
a] *Argent, crusilly gules* – Cavalcanti, Florence
b] *Azure, fleuretty* (alternatively, *semy of fleurs-de-lys*) *or* – France ancient
c] *Argent, 3 bars gules, a bend of France* – Gentien, marquis d'Erigné, Anjou.

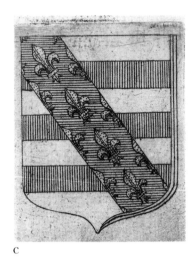

a   b   c

have been assigned to each son, and should be placed so that it is obvious that the *cadency mark* is not part of the arms but a mark of difference. In Scotland a system devised by R.R. Stodart, the last Lyon Clerk Depute, (from 1864 to 1890) is now generally used.

Some popular small charges

To complete this section we will look at two small charges, the *billet*, a rectangular piece, and the *roundle*, as its name suggests a spherical or circular one. *Roundles* come in all colours and each has been given a special name: those of metal, the *bezant* or gold coin from Byzantium, and the silver *plate* (Latin *plata*), together with the *fountain* or *syke* (a well: *a roundle barry wavy argent and azure*), the red *torteau* or *gastel* (a kind of cake or jam-tart), and the blue *hurt* (from Old French *heurt*, a blunt blow making a bruise), should logically be depicted as discs; the black *pellet*, *ogress* or *gunstone*, the green *pomeis* or *pomme* (apple), and the *orange* as spheres. Though there are names for purple and sanguine roundles, the editors of Boutell's *Heraldry* consider that they should be blazoned as *a roundle purpure* or *sanguine* – indeed, it is not incorrect to blazon a *plate*, for instance, as *a roundle argent*.

Both *billets* and *roundles* are frequently scattered (*semy*) over a field; in that case one blazons either *azure, billetty, a lion rampant or*, or *azure, semy of billets, a lion rampant or* (Nassau).[5] Some roundles form a specific adjective, e.g., *bezanty, platy,* and *pomety*; *hurty* is found, but *semy of hurts*, like *semy of fountains*, is more euphonic, while the remaining two, *semy de torteaux* and *semy d'oranges*, keep nearer to French form.

Other common strewn or powdered fields are *gouté, gutty, goutty*, derived from Old French *goutte*, from Latin *gutta*, a drop; and as with roundles, specific near-French terms are used: *goutty d'or, goutty d'eau* (silver rain-drops), *goutty de sang* (drops of blood), *goutty de larmes* (blue tear-drops), *goutty de poix* (drops of pitch or tar), and *goutty d'huile* (drops of green olive oil).

Crusilly means covered in *cross-crosslets*, that is, Latin crosses with each arm also crossed; and in *crusilly fitchy* the vertical arm ends in a point which can be stuck into the ground.

A field covered in fleurs-de-lys is termed *semy de lys, fleury* or *flory*, with the diminutive *fleureté, fleuretty, floretty*, as in the old arms of France, which were changed not long after 1328, when the last King of the direct line died and Edward III of England claimed the throne. One should notice that in all contemporary representations of this field it looks as if it has been cut out of a larger rectangular piece of material, so that part flowers are depicted at the edges and at the base. This is the correct form, and should be employed with all *semy* fields.

Early instances of *fleury* shields

During the 250 years or so that the *Chansons de geste* were popular in French-speaking Western Europe, both Frankish and Saracen *fleury* shields are very frequently mentioned. In the Bodleian Library manuscript of the *Chanson de Roland*, which is contemporary with the first Crusade – around 1100 – the Frankish Guineman attacks a pagan and strikes him on his *targe ki est flurie*. In the *Chanson des Saisnes* (Saxons, who because they are not Christian are treated as Saracens), written by Jehan Bodel at the very end of the twelfth century, Charlemagne strikes Dialas, a pagan prince, *sor la targe florie* (line 7359); later, after the deaths of his father and elder brother, Dialas comes over to the Christian side and is given new arms in the Frankish style:

> . . . .i. escu *paint a flor*
> a .iiii. *lionciaus rampanz* par grant vigor (lines 7877–8),

that is, a shield *semy of flowers, with four lions rampant*.

It is not altogether clear whether these flowers were fleurs-de-lys or rosettes. Both charges were certainly used by Muslims, e.g., the *amir* Najm ad-din Mahmud (d. 1349/50): *argent, a fleur-de-lys and a chief gules*, on a glass lamp in the Royal Scottish Museum, Edinburgh. Of the members of the family of Qalaun, which provided eleven *mamluk* sultans of Egypt and Syria

Fig.22 An example of an Islamic *rank* or blason of the mid 14th century, which could well have been the arms of a contemporary western knight.

Fig.23 Two examples of the use of the rose or rosette: *opposite*, the late 13th-century Islamic insignia of Kafur on a mosque lamp, and, *below*, the arms of the Franconian family of Bappenberg (Petra Sancta).

between 1280 and 1390, some favoured the fleur-de-lys and others the six-petalled red rosette. The Rasulid sultans of Yaman, as well as the personal *trianguly* insignia that we have noticed already, used as their royal arms *argent, a five-petalled rosette gules*. In the Museum is a glass lamp decorated with the arms of the eunuch Shibl ad-daula Kafur (d. 1285): *gules, a six-petalled rosette argent*.

It is interesting that when Dialas is given Frankish arms they are charged with both flowers (almost certainly fleurs-de-lys) and lions. The Muslims called the fleur-de-lys *faransisiya*, Frankish, for it was the charge of both France and Florence (which was in close trading connection with Islam). In the *Prise d'Orenge* (late twelfth century) a Saracen lady arms the hero William with equipment from a chest in her room; round his neck he hangs

un fort escu *listé, a un lion d'or fu coroné* (line 954),

a strong shield with *a bordure and a lion crowned or*. More information of the same type comes from *La Bataille Loquifer* (*c.* 1230): Saracens pretending to be merchants offer for sale hauberks and helms and *escus a lion* (line 50). This was thought by both the author and the Saracens to be the typical Frankish charge.

Evidence from *Les plus anciennes armoiries françaises* of seals and enamels before 1300, and from the earliest English rolls of arms, shows that

Fig.24 Roundle of Shihab ad-din Ahmad.

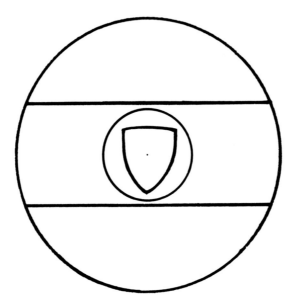

geometrically divided shields are by far the commonest, but that the lion heads the list of animals and the eagle that of birds. It is perhaps no coincidence that the same pattern emerges in the insignia of Islam up to about 1320; with the rosette (which may well have originated in the Far East), the three most popular non-official charges which are not *tamgas* (tribal emblems) are the fleur-de-lys, the lion and the eagle.

Exceptions to the rule of tincturing

So far we have dealt only with examples in which colour is placed on metal or *vice versa*. One will find in many books on Heraldry the statement that this must be so; and then the arms of the Crusader Kingdom of Jerusalem (early: *argent, a cross pommy between four plain crosslets or;* later the cross is *potent*) are mentioned (as recently as 1957) as a well known breach of the colour rule, so that the arms of the Holy City might occupy a unique position in Heraldry!

Neither Islam nor the *Chansons de geste* pay any attention to this 'rule'. On a glass lamp in the Metropolitan Museum, New York, are the insignia of Shihab ad-din Ahmad, commissioner of the Army from 1319–27: *argent, on a fesse gules, a round tray of the field* (i.e., argent) *charged with a pointed shield or*, and on a standard head from Istanbul, the top third of those of the mamluk Barquq, at one time viceroy of Syria (d. 1473), are *or, a napkin argent*.

In the *Chanson des Saisnes*, Berart de Montdidier is knighted by his uncle Charlemagne and given the arms of his father (line 1792): 'the field is white with a lion of beaten gold'. In the *Enfances Ogier* (from the last quarter of the thirteenth century) the father, Thierry d'Ardenne, has, in lines 5115–6:

> Armes ot beles et de riche façon,
> *Blanches* estoient, s'i ot *d'or un lyon.*

> Wonderful arms of a rich fashion,
> Sparkling *white, a golden lion thereon.*

In the earlier twelfth-century *Chanson des Chétifs*, a crusader, Ricars de Calmont, arms himself with a shield (lines 767–8);

> Orlés estoit d'azur, et d'argent bien floris,
> Une crois i ot d'or par sisne Jesu Cris

> Argent flory, and an orle of blue,
> With a golden cross for Our Lord so true,

arms very like those of Jerusalem.

In Appendix F (p.752) of his treatise Mr Woodward, who must be allowed the last word on this matter, mentions 'a couple of dozen instances' of arms, either metal on metal or colour on colour; these are all listed in Rietstap's *Armorial Général* and include *argent, a lion or* (Doro of Venice), *purpure, two reindeer's horns in saltire, tips downwards, gules* (Krogendantz of Norway), arms that would be extremely difficult to make out in battle; and the ancient arms of the 'premier baron chrétien' Montmorency from the Ile de France, *or, a cross argent.*

'I therefore humbly think', concludes Mr Woodward, 'I have proved my case, and that future compilers of books on Heraldry should "gang warily" if they are to avoid the imputation of ignorance when they talk of the arms of JERUSALEM, etc., as "the only instance" of the violation of this rule.'

Fig.25 A party of Norman mounted knights charge Saxon *huscarls*. Note the geometrically decorated shields of the invaders and the plain shields and banner of Harold's troops. *Courtesy of Phaidon Press*

CHAPTER II

THE ORIGINS OF ARMORY

The obvious starting point for any discussion of the origins of Armory is the Bayeux Tapestry. This famous stretch of embroidery was most probably commissioned by William I's uterine brother Odo, Bishop of Bayeux, to be displayed in his new cathedral, dedicated in 1077. It may well have been produced by Saxon artists of the Canterbury school. This agrees with what we know of the career of Bishop Odo, who was the largest landowner in Kent until he was deprived of his English lands in 1082. The prominence of Bayeux and of Odo in the work itself leads one to discard the fanciful story that it was made by the women of William's wife Queen Matilda![6]

The accoutrement of warriors, their armour, weapons, and in particular their banners, are well observed and, within the limitations of the medium, accurately portrayed. The civilian costumes, however, are in many cases copied from earlier models and are therefore quite anachronistic. In another matter the embroiderers are constantly at fault: that is, in the representation of the obvious maleness of the warriors' stallions.

In Wace's *Roman de Rou* (history of Rollo-Hrolfr, the first ruler of Normandy), which the author started late in life in about 1160, is a curious passage: we are assured that it was reported to him by his father, who was aware of the knights' departure from Normandy, that

> . . tuit orent fait conoissances,
> Que Normant altre coneüst
> Qu'entrepresure n'i eüst,
> Que Normant Normant n'oceït,
> Ne Normant altre ne ferist.[7]

> They all had individual signs,
> That Normans might their fellows know,
> Avoiding all confusion so
> That Normans never would a Norman slay,
> Or by mistake their allies flay.

It is my contention, therefore, that shields may also be represented in a rather archaic way. I do not go so far as to say that heraldry was used by the Normans in 1066, but I think it is wrong to insist so definitely, on the evidence of the Bayeux Tapestry, that it was still in the state of anarchy it appears to be.

An early knighting

The first authenticated example of a shield which satisfies the criteria laid down in the first paragraph of this book is that presented to Geoffrey, Count of Anjou, when he was knighted by his father-in-law Henry I of England, at Whitsuntide 1127, in Rouen. The fifteen-year-old count was accompanied by five barons and twenty-five pages. John of Tours, a monk at Marmoutier, who wrote the *Historia Goffredi Plantagenistae*, describes the ceremony in very flowery Latin:

> 'Arising from the bath, Geoffrey, the noble offspring of the count of Anjou, put on a fine linen garment next to his flesh, assumed a mantle woven with gold over that and donned a mantle of state dyed with purple and the blood of the murex,[8] was clothed with silken leggings, and his feet fitted with shoes that had small golden lions on their surface.
>
> 'His companions who were awaiting the honour of knighthood with him were all clothed in linen and purple.
>
> 'The horses were brought, the arms were brought . . .
>
> 'He was clothed with an incomparable cuirass, woven with double links, unable to be pierced by any lance or javelin blow. He was shod with iron leggings also of double weave; golden shoes were fitted to his feet. A shield, bearing small gold lions figured on it, was hung round his neck; on his head was placed a helm gleaming with many a precious stone . . .
>
> 'He was brought his ashen spear . . .
>
> 'Lastly a sword was brought to him from the royal treasury, where it was recorded to have lain long, in the making of which the chiefest of smiths, Wayland, had spent much time and effort.'

Geoffrey died in 1151, and his funeral plaque from Le Mans cathedral, now in the Musée Tessé, shows the same arms: *azure*, probably *six lions or*, which were used by his grandson William Longespée, a bastard of Henry II by (reputedly) the fair Rosamund. In 1196 William's half-brother Richard I gave him Ela, Countess of Salisbury, in marriage, with the Earldom. He died in 1226 and was buried in the Cathedral, at the laying of whose foundations he had assisted six years before. On the shield of his effigy the six lions can be clearly seen, and his arms passed to his descendants.

A Muslim Lordship is confirmed

This description of Geoffrey's knighting is like others in the *Chansons de geste*,[9] and in many cases the language of biography and that of poetry are very close.

Fig.26 Two mamluks from the metalwork bowl
known as the 'Baptistère de Saint Louis'.
Courtesy of the Musée du Louvre

It is interesting to compare the account written by the Arab historian
Abu'l-Fida' of how his cousin al-Muzaffar Mahmud was confirmed in his
rank of lord of Hamah in 1284 by Sultan Qalaun. The sultan sent him '. . . a
diploma which constituted him sultan of Hamah, of El Ma-arra and of
Barin. The apparel of honour which accompanied this document consisted
of an over-robe of red satin embroidered in gold, a fur cape of miniver, a
loose cape of beaver, an under-coat of yellow satin, the cloth for a turban of
nine folds, breeches brocaded in gold, a gold belt, a sword furnished in gold,
a quiver, an amber box, a hood with a gold border, and a pair of underpants.
'The sultan also sent him his sultanic insignia, which consisted of a flag
decorated with the streamers of a sultan, a horse with a golden saddle, a
yellow silk neck-covering for the horse, and a horsetrapper.'
Unfortunately no arms are mentioned; but we know from other sources
that Muzaffar, like his father Muhammad, whom he succeeded in 1284,
bore insignia *bendy and a chief*. The historian, when he was confirmed as ruler
of Hamah in 1320 by Qalaun's son and successor, an-Nasir Muhammad,
used the same arms, the chief uncoloured (perhaps white is intended), the
bends either ten or twelve in number, gold, red, gold, black, gold, etc.

The genealogical table on p.45 shows the family of the descendants of Ayyub, who from around 1170 to 1250 ruled an area stretching from the Nile to the southern borders of modern Turkey. The most important member of this family was Saladin, the chivalrous enemy of Richard the Lion-Heart, and it was he more than any other who halted the advance of the Crusading armies. The allegorical story of Richard splitting an anvil with his great sword and Saladin severing a cushion with his razor-sharp scimitar shows the fundamental differences between the armies of Christ and of Islam.

It is interesting at this point to consider the 'Saracen' poet and chronicler Abu'l-Mahasin Yusuf's definition of the term *furusiyya* (that is, all branches of hippology: breeding, horse-doctoring, feeding, the lance game, polo, archery, musical rides, hunting and horse-racing, among others) as it applies to jousting. The historian's father Taghribirdi was a distinguished amir, governor when he died in 1412 of Aleppo and Damascus, and we can therefore rely on the testimony of the son.

'*Furusiyya* is something different from bravery and intrepidity, for the brave man overthrows his adversary by sheer courage, while the [true] horseman is one who handles his horse well in the charge and in the retreat and knows all that he needs to know about his horse and his weapons and about how to handle them in accordance with the rules known and established among the masters of this art.'

Though the western knights too were very competent horsemen, the climate, the terrain and the distance from their homelands were all against their ultimate success.

The role of the Crusaders in the development of Armory

So we can see that Heraldry in the West, as exemplified by the arms of Geoffrey of Anjou, was becoming established certainly by the end of the first half of the twelfth century, and that a similar system was used by the Ayyubids of Hamah a hundred and fifty years later.

Is it therefore safe to say that both Christian and Islamic Heraldry was a direct result of the Crusades? In the case of Islam I think the answer is yes – though when we look at the developments in the Middle East we shall see for how short a time the system lasted.

In the West the answer is not so straightforward. One reason put forward by heraldists for the adoption of armorial devices during the twelfth century is the fact that at this time the closed helm became normal wear, and therefore it was impossible to recognise individuals' features. Evidence from

GENEALOGICAL TABLE: THE AYYUBIDS

AYYUB † 1171-2

HAMA

EGYPT & SYRIA

SHAHANSHAH
† c. 1146

SAIF AD-DIN ABU-BAKR † 1216

AL-MUZAFFAR (I) TAQI AD-DIN ʿUMAR
re: 1178–91 (une banière as braies)

MUHAMMAD (I)
re: 1191–1220

SALAH AD-DIN YUSUF
(SALADIN) † 1192-3

AL-KAMIL MUHAMMAD
re: 1218–1238

AL-MUZAFFAR GHAZI
† 1244-5 (a lion facing a man)

AL-KAMIL MUHAMMAD
† c. 1260

AL-MUZAFFAR (II)
re: 1229–1244

Ghazia Khatun =

AS-SALIH AYYUB =
re: 1240–1249

Shajar al-Durr =
re: 1249–1250

AYBAK re: 1252–7
(argent a qashnikir's table gules)

ALI
re: 1257–9

ALI

ABU'L-FIDA' AL-MU'AYYAD
The historian re: 1320–1331
(bendy of 10 gold, red, gold, black, etc.)

TARAN SHAH
re: 1250

MUHAMMAD (II)
re: 1244–1284
(bendy, on a chief a lion)

AL-MUZAFFAR (III)
re: 1284–1298
(bendy & a chief)

MUHAMMAD (III)
re: 1331–

ISMAIL
† 1357

ALI
viv 1374
(bendy of 6 & a chief)

From S. Lane-Poole, *The Mohammadan Dynasties* (1925) and E. de Zambaut *Manuel*, (1927).
Reproduced from The Palestine Exploration Quarterly, 1982/1.

45

Fig.27 Duke William removes his helm. *Courtesy of Phaidon Press*

the Bayeux Tapestry makes this doubtful, for in plate 68 of the Phaidon edition 'Eustace of Boulogne points to William, *who lifts his helm and shows his face to dispel a rumour that he had been killed*' (my italics). This is the open conical helm with a nasal.

Geoffrey was knighted over twenty-five years after the first Crusade, and in this period, immediately prior to the second, a number of heraldic seals make their appearance. The earliest are perhaps those of Waleran, Count of Meulan and Earl of Worcester (d. 1166), where a chequy pattern is evident on his surcoat, saddlecloth and pennon. These checks raise a fundamental question about the date of the origins of heraldry, for several related families close to the French Royal House bear blue and gold chequy arms which seem to originate from the very end of the eleventh century. By looking at the family tree on p.47, one can see that many of the connections of Hugh de Vermandois (viv.1057, d. 1102), a crusader in 1096 and in 1101–2, when he died in Outremer, bore chequy arms (mainly in the royal French colours).

In battle, as an account of the death of the brother of the French King St. Louis will show, it was the *colours* of the arms, rather than the actual design, that mattered. Former writers on this matter may have placed too much emphasis on descent from the family of Vermandois; but it is because Hugh le Grand was a younger son of Henri I, not because he married Adeline de Vermandois, that blue and gold checks were attributed to him. His uncle Robert le Vieux (1031–76) was the first Duke of Burgundy, and we know that the ancient arms of that duchy were *bendy or and azure, a bordure gules*; his great-nephew Robert le Grand was the first Count of Dreux, and he used the blue and gold checks within a *bordure gules*.

Table to show the use of related arms by some descendants of Henri I and their connections

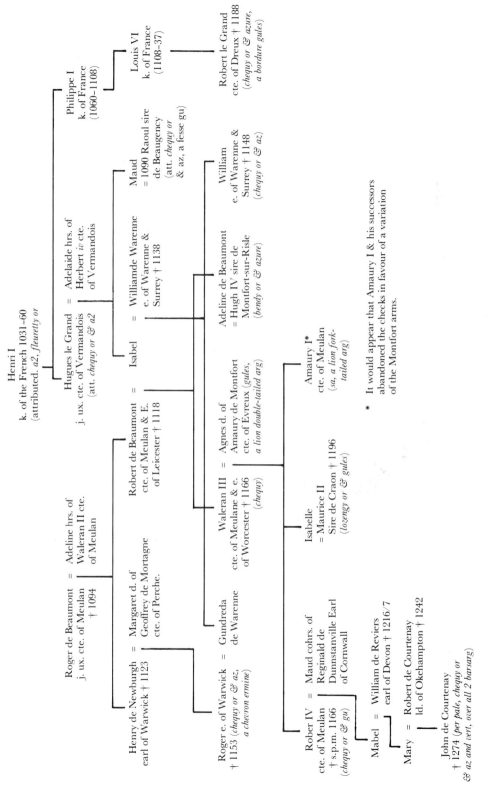

Henri I
k. of the French 1031–60
(attributed. *a2, fleuretty or*)

Hugues le Grand = Adelaide hrs. of
j. ux. cte. of Vermandois   Herbert *iv* cte.
(att. *chequy or & a2*)   of Vermandois

Philippe I
k. of France
(1060–1108)

Louis VI
k. of France
(1108–37)

Robert le Grand
cte. of Dreux † 1188
(*chequy or & azure,
a bordure gules*)

Maud
= 1090 Raoul sire
de Beaugency
(att. *chequy or
& az, a fesse gu*)

Williamde Warenne = Isabel
e. of Warenne &
Surrey † 1138

William
e. of Warenne &
Surrey † 1148
(*chequy or & az*)

Roger de Beaumont = Adeline hrs. of
j. ux. cte. of Meulan   Waleran II cte.
† 1094   of Meulan

Henry de Newburgh = Margaret d. of
earl of Warwick † 1123   Geoffrey de Mortagne
cte. of Perche.

Robert de Beaumont
cte. of Meulan & E.
of Leicester † 1118

Adeline de Beaumont
= Hugh IV sire de
Montfort-sur-Risle
(*bendy or & azure*)

Roger e. of Warwick = Gundreda
† 1153 (*chequy or & az,   de Warenne
a chevron ermine*)

Waleran III = Agnes d. of
cte. of Meulane & e.   Amaury de Montfort
of Worcester † 1166   cte. of Evreux (*gules,
(*chequy*)   a lion double-tailed arg*)

Amaury I*
cte. of Meulan
(*sa, a lion fork-
tailed arg*)

Isabelle
= Maurice II
Sire de Craon † 1196
(*lozengy or & gules*)

Rober IV = Maud cohrs. of
cte. of Meulan   Reginald de
† s.p.m. 1166   Dunnstanville Earl
(*chequy or & gu*)   of Cornwall

Mabel = William de Reviers
earl of Devon † 1216/7

Mary = Robert de Courtenay
ld. of Okehampton † 1242

John de Courtenay
† 1274 (*per pale, chequy or
& az and vert, over all 2 barsarg*)

* It would appear that Amaury I & his successors
  abandoned the checks in favour of a variation
  of the Montfort arms.

* Amaury I*

Main references: G. Sirjean, *Encyclopédie Généalogique* (1960 ff)
J.B. Burke, *Dormant & Extinct Peerages* (1866)

47

In the *Entrée d'Espagne*, of about 1340–50, Roland, the nephew of Charlemagne (who in all the *Chansons* in which he appears is more important than any son of the Emperor) bears *quarterly or and azure*. In lines 1671–2 his shield (or perhaps his gonfalon) is described thus:

> . . . . . le quartier resplant
> d'un clier colors celestre et d'or lusant;[10]
> > one quarter glows
> with shining gold and the bright heaven's hue;

in lines 4345–6 he sets up over a captured pagan city

> . . . . l'ensaigne San Donis
> e le quartier d'or e de color bis;
> > the standard of Saint Dennis old
> with the quartered blue and gold.

The author knew that the arms of France were

> . . . . cele ensaigne
> O le flors d'or baloie en celestre campaigne,
> > the flag where golden flowers weave
> On the blue and heavenly field,

and he perhaps knew also that cadets of France adopted in various forms the livery colours to create new designs. If this had not been the case, the quartered shield for Roland would have made no sense to the audience.

Throughout Western Europe the call to arms to fight the infidel and gain a sure reward in heaven was virtually irresistible, especially to those who had not an assured reward in land or office here on earth. Whatever the rights and wrongs of the Holy Wars, they had a profound influence on the life of people from all social classes, and those who did not take the Cross were to a greater or lesser extent prepared to do so.

Arms and the tournament

Surrogate warfare, in the form of mêlées and tournaments, was the answer to the Church's constant appeals for an end to battles between fellow-Christians. Though against tournaments too the Church fulminated, they were a very necessary training for the young knight, and provided, often too exactly, the dangers of the genuine thing.

It was in fact against this dangerous element – against the mortal sin of wantonly hazarding or throwing away one's own life or that of a fellow man

– that the Church chiefly preached and levelled her prohibitions. Other sins – those of pride, extravagance, loose living, drinking and gambling – were closely allied to the mimic battle in the eyes of the Church, and churchmen such as Archbishop Wichmann of Magdeburg were prepared to wield excommunication even against their own relatives who took part.

Other churchmen, like the lay aristocrats, felt a morbid fascination for the waste, the blood, the dust, and the wreckage in both human lives and rich material objects, that were its results.[11] On the one hand the tournament was a necessary form of training and in its ritual a civilising influence on the participants; on the other a brutal waste of the time, the wealth and the lives of knights who should have been engaged in fighting the Saracens.

As late as 1559 Henri II, King of France, died some days after a formal joust because a shiver from the lance of Gabriel de Montgomery of the *Garde Ecossaise* penetrated his eye. Among other notable casualties was Robert, Count of Clermont and youngest son of St. Louis, who in his first tournament in 1278, when he was only twenty-two, 'weighed down by his arms, and being struck hard and frequently on the head with mallets, confused by troubling of the brain, fell into perpetual witlessness' (Guillaume de Nangis, *Gesta Philippi Regis*). He survived, however, until 1318, outlived one of his sons, and through the other, Louis, first Duke of Bourbon, became the ancestor of Henri IV.

Geoffrey, Duke of Brittany, the fourth and perhaps the most unfilial of the sons of Henry II of England, was thrown in a tournament outside Paris and died a few days later, on 19 August 1186, of a fever brought on by his injuries; as Alfred Duggan rightly comments in *Devil's Brood*, 'if he had been killed outright he would have died excommunicate and been forbidden a Christian burial' – a thing awful to contemplate in those times.

A generation later, Gilbert Marshal, 4th Earl of Pembroke, died in the same way, at Hertford in 1241. It is curious that five brothers in turn all inherited this Earldom and died without issue; their father, William Marshal, was a poor squire whose rise to fame he owed largely to his prowess in the tournament. He knew well the sons of Henry II, and was rewarded by Richard I at his coronation with marriage to Isabel, heiress of Richard 'Strongbow' de Clare and the Earldom of Pembroke.

In the *Histoire de Guillaume le Maréchal*, his competence is noticed as early as 1174 by Bon-Abbé, sire de Rougé, who asks Johan de Soleigni who he is. In lines 1474ff. Johan replies:

C'est Guill. Li Mareschals . . .
Si cuit que vos n'eüstes unkes
Nul bacheler plus seit sans gile.
Sis escus est de Tankarvile.

That is William Marshal, sire,
who I believe of all your squires
is the one who knows least guile.
The arms he bears are Tankarvile.

In the mêlée where individual achievement gained prizes it was perhaps more important to be clearly recognised than on the battlefield. It is here, therefore, that I believe we should look for the origins of arms, and also for the origins of the control exercised by the Heralds over the adoption and wearing of arms.

It is very possible that the custom of displaying one's arms before the tournament, at which time the heralds made an inspection, led to the present arrangement of the full achievement.

Duke René of Anjou, the father of Margaret, Henry VI's unfortunate queen, was a nobleman with more titular than actual power. He wrote much, both poetry and prose, he painted, illuminated and designed; in his treatise usually known as the *Livre des Tournois du Roi René*,[12] he lays down strict rules about the tournament:

> 'All Princes, Lords, Barons, Knights and Squires that intend to tourney, you are all expected to appear at the lodgings on the fourth day before the day of the Tourney, to display your Blasons, under pain of not being received at the said Tourney. The arms will be thus. The crest must be on a piece of boiled leather, at least a finger thick; and the said piece of leather should contain the whole top of the helm, and the said piece shall be covered by the lambrequin bearing the owner's arms, and on the said lambrequin at the very top the said crest should be set, and around it there shall be a wreath of colours as the Tourneyer wishes.'

The crests are to be set up so that the judges and ladies may walk around them, and a herald is to be present to identify their owners' names.

In the illustration which accompanies this text, squires stand behind the helmets, holding banners of the combatants' arms. Though these squires are wearing conventional clothes, it is thought that on some occasions they were disguised as beasts, birds or wodwoses (wild men), and that supporters originated in this way.

Another, less romantic, but perhaps more likely, theory is that they were originally nothing but space-fillers between the escutcheon and crest and the circular inscription around the rim of a seal. Traditionally, only temporal peers have hereditary supporters; life peers, and Knights of the Garter, the Thistle and St. Patrick, with Knights Grand Cross or Knights Grand Commanders of other orders, have personal supporters only. There are some exceptions: in Scotland clan chieftains who are not peers have hereditary supporters, and some baronets (both of Ulster and of Nova Scotia) have been granted them.

Heraldry and politics

The *stemma* of the heraldist René is a good example of the use of Heraldry for political propaganda: his shield is *Quarterly of five*[13] *1. argent, three bars gules* (Hungary ancient); *2. azure, fleuretty or, a label of three points gules* (Anjou-Sicile); *3. argent, a cross potent between four cross crosslets or* (Jerusalem); *4. azure, fleuretty or, a bordure gules* (Anjou); *5. azure, crusilly two barbels addorsed or* (Bar). An inescutcheon *or, three palets gules* (Aragon).

By reference to his family tree we can see that he had no claim to the throne of Hungary, though this had at one time belonged to a line of Anjou-Sicile. The second, third and fourth quarters also come from his paternal ancestry, but there was never any question of his exercising sovereign rights over either Jerusalem or Sicily. The dukedom of Bar was an inheritance of his grandmother's, and Aragon (of which he was the official claimant between 1467 and 1470) of his mother's. The arms of the kingdom to which he had some hope of succeeding appear therefore in the centre; up to 1453, when his first wife Isabelle died, the arms of Lorraine could have occupied that position, though a manuscript illumination of *c.*1435-6 [14] shows the arms of Lorraine (*or, on a bend gules three alerions of the field*) in René's sixth quarter.

René is saying, in effect, 'I should be ruler of all these fiefs'. Edward III of England was doing exactly the same when he placed the French fleurs-de-lys in the first and fourth quarters of the English arms. He thus registered his claim to that kingdom, through his mother Isabelle, the eventual heiress of Philippe IV, as being more valid than that of the Valois, Philippe VI.

However, it was not unknown for a knight to bear another's arms, not as a political gesture, that is, to signify fealty, but out of deference to an important personage. We have seen that William Marshal in his youth bore the arms of his tutor William de Tankarvile, hereditary chamberlain of Normandy: *gules, an escutcheon argent within an orle of eight angemmes or.*[15]

51

Matthew Paris[16] records his death in 1219 (*Obiit comes Willelmus Marescallus senior*) and his reversed shield is *party per pale or and vert, a lion rampant queue fourchée gules*. These are the arms of the Marshalcy, which were used in turn by his three eldest sons, William junior, Richard, and Gilbert, who succeeded him in that office, and eventually passed to Hugh Bigod, Earl of Norfolk, who married Maud, the senior coheiress after her brothers. From the *Song of the Siege of Caerlaverock* (1300), we know that the family, as opposed to the official, arms borne by a cousin, another William, were *gules, a bend engrailed* (or *of lozenges*) *or*:

> E Guillems li Marescaus
> Dont en Irlande ot la baillie
> La bende de or engreelie
> Portoit en la rouge baniere.

> The Marshal, baron William,
> Lord of the Irish shore,
> A bend engrailed of gold he bore,
> Upon a banner red.

Joinville, in his *Histoire de Saint Louis*, notes that when the crusaders arrived in Egypt in the spring of 1249,

> 'On our left side arrived the Count of Jaffa, who was cousin german to the Count of Montbeliard and of the lineage of Joinville. He made the most noble show arriving, for his galley was all painted above and below deck with shields of his arms, which are *gold, a cross patty gules*; he had a good 300 rowers in his galley, and each of these had a targe of his arms, and with each targe went a pennoncel of his arms, worked in gold.'

It was more normal for the knights and squires of a mesnie not to wear the complete arms of their lords, but the livery colours and a badge. We have seen that sons and brothers difference the arms of the head of the family, for this avoids such confusion, whether real or induced it is hard to say, as Joinville reports to have occurred when the leader of the Saracens 'took the coat of the Count of Artois who had been killed in the battle and showed it to all the Saracens and told them it was the coat of arms of the King.'

Christian and Islamic knightly practice

It is worth noting here that the wearing of a surcoat over armour was not a general rule in the twelfth century either for Muslims or for Christians.

53

Usamah ibn-Munqidh in his *Memoirs*[17] describes two instances: 'One of our troops, a Kurd named Mayyah, smote a Frankish knight with a lance, which made a piece of the link in his coat of chain mail penetrate into his abdomen, and killed him.

'A few days later the Franks made a raid against us. Mayyah, who had just been married, went out to meet them in full armour, but wearing over his coat of mail a red garment of his bridal clothes, making himself especially conspicuous. A Frankish knight smote him with a lance and killed him (may Allah's mercy rest upon his soul!) O, how close to his funeral was his wedding!'

Usamah also tells a story against himself: 'One of their horsemen hastened towards me, displaying his colours on a green and yellow silk tunic, under which I thought was no coat of mail. I therefore let him alone until he passed me. Then I applied the spurs to my mare, which leaped over the wall, and I smote him with my lance. He bent sideways so much that his head reached the stirrups, his shield and his lance fell out of his hand, and his helmet off his head. By that time we had reached the infantry. He then resumed his position, erect in the saddle, having had linked mail under his tunic; my lance did not wound him!'

In his introduction, Professor Hitti calls Usamah of Shayzar 'a warrior, a hunter, a gentleman, a poet and a man of letters'. Writing in about 1170 with clearness of mind and a vivid eye for detail, he remembered what had happened to him twenty-five years previously when travelling under safe-conduct. 'The King (may Allah not have mercy on his soul!)', Baldwin II of Jerusalem (re.1142–62), had sent out his men to break up Usamah's ship and then confiscated everything, explaining that that was the custom of the land. He then gave the Arab five hundred dinars so that he might continue his journey . . . 'The safety of my children, my brothers' children and our harem made the loss of money which we suffered a comparatively easy thing to endure – with the exception of the books, which were four thousand volumes, all of the most valuable kind. Their loss has left a heartsore that will stay with me to the last day of my life . . .'

This short digression tells us much about the character of Usamah. He is without doubt one of the most reliable and intelligent commentators of the period, who can review from his old age with some compassion and understanding, but at the same time with flashes of bitterness, the fierce struggles of his youth, not only between Muslim and Christian, but also between Arab and Turk.

Jean Sire de Joinville, though I doubt if he wrote poetry, could well be described in the same way as Usamah. Unlike his pious and bigoted King

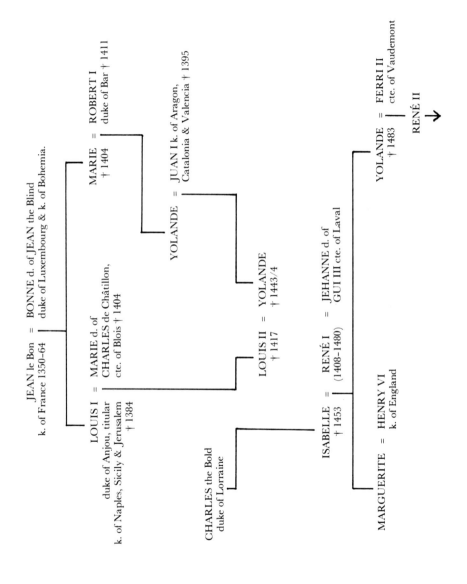

JEAN le Bon = BONNE d. of JEAN the Blind
k. of France 1350–64   duke of Luxembourg & k. of Bohemia.

LOUIS I = MARIE d. of
duke of Anjou, titular   CHARLES de Châtillon,
k. of Naples, Sicily & Jerusalem   cte. of Blois † 1404
† 1384

MARIE = ROBERT I
† 1404   duke of Bar † 1411

YOLANDE = JUAN I k. of Aragon,
Catalonia & Valencia † 1395

LOUIS II = YOLANDE
† 1417   † 1443/4

CHARLES the Bold
duke of Lorraine

ISABELLE = RENÉ I = JEHANNE d. of
† 1453   (1408–1480)   GUI III cte. of Laval

YOLANDE = FERRI II
† 1483   cte. of Vaudemont

RENÉ II

MARGUERITE = HENRY VI
k. of England

55

Fig.29 Windsock banner – an artist's impression.

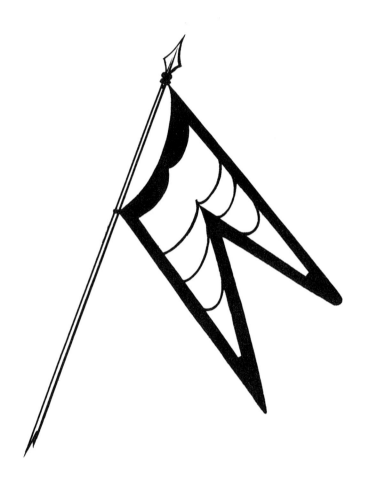

and friend, St. Louis, he had an open and inquisitive mind; he derived great pleasure from learning about such people as the Berbers and the Assassins, in the same way as he was interested in the heraldry of the Muslims and in the finding of a fossilised fish.

He too dictated his memoirs, some fifty-five years after the events of the seventh Crusade, which started from Paris in the summer of 1248. Though he tends sometimes to repeat himself, his views, where they can be checked, are sound and accurate. If he makes a statement that seems a little unlikely, it is wise to pay attention to it, for he was close to the King and in a much better position to know the truth than the writers of *Chansons de geste* or historians such as Ambroise.

An observation made by Ambroise between 1191 and 1196 and recorded in his *Estoire de la Guerre Sainte*, which was translated into Latin under the title *Itinerarium Regis Ricardi*, has haunted historians of Islamic insignia until recently: he says in effect that Taqi ad-din Umar, the nephew of Saladin, bore as his banner *a pair of trousers*:

L'amiralz Dequedin
un des parenz de Salahedin
Qui ot portrait en sa baniere
enseignes d'estrange maniere
Ço estoit une baniere as braies
c'erent ses enseignes veraies.

There the amir Taqadin
a close relation of great Saladin
displayed in a most curious manner
a pair of drawers upon his banner.

This was almost certainly a windsock banner, as shown in Fig.29.[18] Ambroise's distorted view of it was very much influenced by Westerners' views of Islam.

Taqi ad-din was of the same family as the rulers of Hamah, who, as we have seen on p.43, bore *bendy and a chief*. As witnesses of heraldic practice, the writers of *chansons de geste* should always be treated with great caution.

The following examples show how easy it was to be misled. In the thirteenth-century *Foucon de Candie*, the same Ayyubid prince rides up with his 'lance levee, son confanon porprin'. In the early *Chanson de Jérusalem*, written in about 1130–40 and later worked over, Cornumarans, the historical Kerbogha (Kawam ad-daula Karbuka) is given a different shield on no less than five occasions: in line 1388, he arms himself with *.i. escu vert et bis*, in line 3764 he seizes his *escu a argent*, in line 5139 he is struck on his *targe florie*, in line 5255 his *escu a or* is buckled and crushed, and when he is killed he is carried away *dedesor son escu* (colour not named)!

Developments in Mamluk insignia

This is not an isolated example: in the earlier *Chansons* there is no consistency in the description of Saracen shields. Yet Joinville, writing about the aftermath of the Battle of Mansourah in February-April 1250, when the French were defeated and King Louis captured, thought that there was a system:

'The arms of the sultan were gold, and such arms that the sultan bore, these young lads bore as well; and they were called *bahariz* (literally, 'men of the sea' – so-called because these mamluks lived on Rauda Island at the mouth of the Nile). When their beards started to grow, the sultan knighted them and they continued to bear his arms except that they were differenced, in that they had crimson charges such as rosettes, red bends or birds or other charges that they placed on their gold arms just as they pleased.'

As has been mentioned in 'Saracen and Crusader Heraldry in Joinville's History of Saint Louis',[19] Joinville is writing about what he saw in 1249–50, that is, in the period when these Bahri mamluks were replacing the last Ayyubids as Sultans in Egypt and Syria. However, it is not until the reign of al-Malik Kitbugha (1294–6) that we find evidence of this kind of system.

The Muslim historian Al-Dhahabi says: 'While amir he (Kitbugha) carried this coat of arms [*or, a fesse and a cup in base gules*], while king yellow banners.'[20] Two of his brother mamluks, who had been educated with him and became his companions at the military academy, Kujkhun (d. 1338/9) and Lajin, who deposed him in 1296 and ruled until 1299, bore *or, a fesse gules*. Other leading amirs had similar blazons: Arghun (d. 1347/8) *or, on a fesse gules a napkin of the field*; Aslam, the armour-bearer (d. 1346), *or, on a fesse gules a scimitar of the field*, and another armour-bearer, Qijlis (d. 1330), *gules, on a fesse plain a scimitar sable banded argent*.

These mamluk slaves were for the most part Turks or Circassians who had been bought at an early age. There was a flourishing trade in healthy, good-looking boys, and, contrary to general belief, they were neither exclusively homosexual nor eunuchs – the latter seldom joined the military *élite*. They were given a thorough grounding in the Qu'ran and were highly trained as mounted warriors; if successful, they became amirs and could attain the highest rank, that of Sultan, a position that commanded more respect even than the Caliph, who ranked as an amir in charge of religious matters.

Mamluks who had been brought up together formed close-knit units within the military caste, and, for example, Lajin, though he deposed Kujkhun from the Sultanship, had very real feelings of affection for him.

It would seem unlikely that Joinville knew of developments in amiral insignia at the end of the thirteenth century, and I think we can well accept that they took place about fifty years earlier than has hitherto been thought.

Surviving objects from Egypt and Syria decorated with armorial insignia show us four definite stages of development, of which that mentioned by Joinville is the second. These are shown in the illustration on p.60.

The Muslim chronicler Ahmad al-Qalqashandi tells us in the *Subh al-Asha* (advice to civil servants), completed in 1412, that 'it was customary for every amir . . . big or small, to have a special blazon according to his choice or preference . . . It was applied in colour above the doors of his houses and

Fig.30 The mosque lamp of Qijlis.

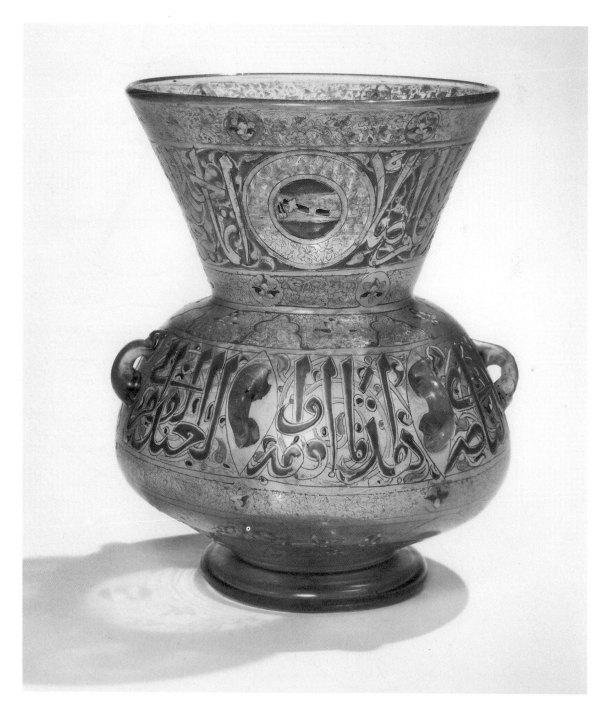

Fig.31 Four stages of amiral insignia:
a] Up to *c.*1300, single element blazons;
b] From *c.*1300 or earlier to *c.*1400: the
introduction of chiefs and fesses;
c] *c.*1400–70: tripartite insignia, each part
charged;
d] *c.*1470–1517 (the Ottoman conquest):
composite blazons for 'the men of the pen' and
'the men of the sword'.
It must be emphasised that these dates, except
the last, are approximate. Blazons of one type
may be found in other periods.

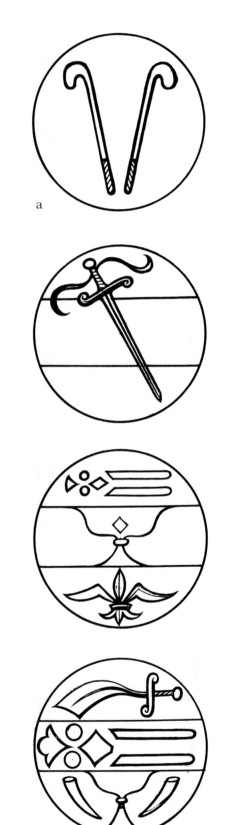

a

b

c

d

Fig.32 The Vaughan grant of arms. This grant 'fait et donne a Londres le jour de saint Ambroise . . . en lan du regne du roy Henry le septiesme nře [nostre] tres redoubte & souuerain seigneur le septiesme' is very important as it confirms the power of the Heralds to grant nobility in the name of the sovereign.

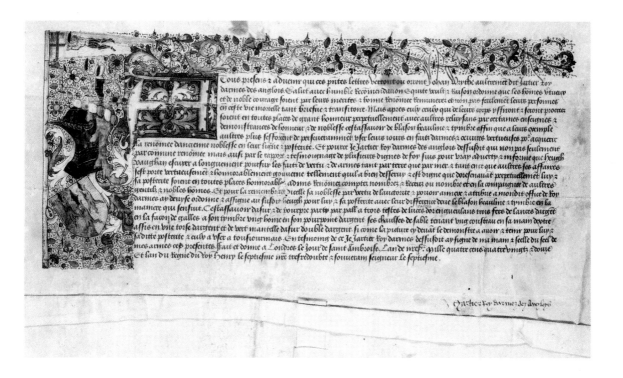

other buildings, such as sugar factories and granaries, and on his boats and other possessions. Also in coloured cloth or wool on his horse blankets and camel cloths and embroidered on similar articles, and sometimes even on swords, bows, harness for his horses and other things.'

There is no mention of their blazons on shields, and as far as I know there is no manuscript which represents Muslim warriors with such a thing.

Illustrations from the *Story of Vargue and Golsah*[21] are reminiscent of the descriptions in the *Chansons*. Bordures, checks and rosettes abound, but there is no continuity. Golsah is given at one time *azure, fleuretty and a bordure or*, at another, *a rosette and a bordure*, and on a third occasion *checks*.

Escus as well as *targes* are portrayed, and colours, shapes and patterns are chosen by the artist on grounds of composition, not realism. We must therefore look elsewhere for the charges of Islamic insignia.

The control of Arms

We have seen that in Europe, by about 1300, heralds had gained some control over the adoption and differencing of arms, and by 1484, when the

College of Arms was given a grant of incorporation by Richard III, this control became officially recognised.

In the Near East this process seems to have been in reverse: Abu'l-Mahasin, referring to an event which had taken place in the first half of the thirteenth century, when the Sultan of Egypt al-Malik Ayyub (re.1240–44) dubbed Aybak an amir, says 'he gave him the figure of a table' – or perhaps more correctly a tray – 'as his blazon'. However, Qalqashandi at the beginning of the following century pays little attention to blazons, as they were no longer one of the privileges controlled by the government.

In the Victoria and Albert is a grant of arms made eight years after the foundation of the College, which can be said to have been the direct cause of a judicial killing: Sir James Parker disputed the right of Hugh Vaughan of Kidwelly, a gentleman usher to Henry VII, to bear arms (granted 7 December 1492) *dasur & de pourpre party per pall a trois testes de luces d'or rasess engueulans trois fers de lances dargent*.[22] Vaughan produced this document, made by John Wrythe, Garter, and the King pronounced that it was as good as an act made by himself. In consequence, at a tournament at Richmond, Hugh Vaughan challenged Sir James and killed him.

The development of Islamic insignia

The early Islamic insignia of which we have a record consist for the most part of one element. The rosette, with a varying number of petals, as we would expect from literary and pictorial sources, is the most common; this is followed, as mentioned above, by the fleuron or fleur-de-lys, the lion, and the eagle. These four charges are perfectly recognisable, though in the case of the lion and to a lesser extent of the eagle the shape is unfamiliar, but they have the same connotations of royalty as they do in the West.

The Muslim palette too contained the same colours; Rukn ad-din Baybars as-Salihi bore *argent, a lion passant gules*, as on the glass goblet in the Museum, and this should be compared with the *lions passant guardant* of his contemporary Henry III of England.

Baybars' honorific Rukn ad-din means *pillar of the faithful*, and as he was a mamluk of al-Malik as-Salih, he bore the distinguishing name as-Salihi, the man or slave of as-Salih; he rose to become Chief of the Corps of Masters of the Robes and the second mamluk Sultan, reigning as al-Malik az-Zahir from 1260 to 1277.

The ruler Baybars succeeded was Aybak; the latter was another amir of al-Malik as-Salih, whose widow Shajar al-Durr he had married in 1249–50 and from whose son he later usurped the sultanate. Aybak reigned from

1252 to 1257, when he was followed by his own son al-Malik Ali, who did not survive long.

When Aybak became Sultan he kept his amiral blazon of *argent, a table gules*: the tinctures are not certain; that of his son we do not know. The table or tray was not strictly a personal blazon but an official one, which was given to the Sultan's Taster (*jashnikir*; see p.125).[23] There were around twenty insignia, of which the following are the most common. A Cupbearer (*saqi*) has a cup, and the Master of the Robes (*jamdar*) a napkin or rhomb; an Armour Bearer (*silahdar*) has a sword, a dagger or a scimitar, the Polomaster (*jukandar*) polosticks, and the Bowman (*bunduqdar*) a bow, sometimes accompanied by one or more arrows. A Secretary (*dawadar*) bore the representation of a penbox, but this is not found in the early period, nor do the polosticks survive into the later one.

Aydamur, 'the Master of the Robes, the Qaimarite', who was viceroy of Syria in 1271–2 and died in 1300, on a basin bears *a napkin* and *a white lion passant sinister*. On the Madrasa Almalikiyya in Jerusalem, and elsewhere, are the insignia of Almalik, a native of Abulstan, who was bought by Baybars in 1277, was polomaster shortly before 1308 and died in 1346/7 – *vert, two polosticks argent* (see above). Of Aydakin, 'the crossbowman', who was *saqi* to al-Malik as-Salih and died in 1285, survives a mosque lamp in the Metropolitan Museum, New York, decorated with his arms, *gules, two bows addorsed or*.

As well as these official insignia, there were of course personal symbols which had much the same significance as those used in the West. The powerful and much-commemorated al-Malik az-Zahir Baybars bore *a lion passant* to signify imperium and strength;[24] it was widely used during the seventeen years of his reign and was inherited by his son al-Malik Baraka-Khan (re.1277–80).

As the lion appears only infrequently after the death of Baraka-Khan, I agree entirely with Dr Meinecke's statement that 'Altogether it is highly probable that the lion as a personal sign was only used by the powerful Sultan az-Zahir Baybars . . . [and his son] . . . All other occurrences are not real blazons but either sultanic symbols or ensigns used only for a limited period . . . and . . . in these cases it was not meant to be a real blazon identifying its holder, but very possibly only a sign of symbolic value and thus merely indicating the imperial or sultanic power.'

Some amirs of Baybars, such as Aydamur al-Jamdar, who bore as well as his official insignia *a lion passant sinister argent*, and Altunbugha (*plain, on a napkin azure a lion passant or*) used the lion in much the same way as the retainers of a Western lord used his badge or some other emblem as livery. A

well-known example of this is the much later Bear-and-Ragged-Staff livery
worn by the cut-throats of Richard Neville, 'the King-Maker', Earl of
Warwick and Salisbury (1428–71).

The lion on the chief of the Ayyubid Muhammad II of Hamah may have
been adopted in rather the same way that noble Italian families took a chief
of Anjou or of the Empire, to show their political allegiance. In this matter,
too, Joinville seems to have early examples. Describing Scecedins (the
Saracen diplomat and army commander Fakhr ad-din ibn Sadr ad-din
al-Shaykh, who died in 1250), he calls him 'the chieftain of the Turks who
was the most esteemed in all heathendom . . . His banner was divided into
three bands and on one of the bands was the arms of the emperor who made
him knight; in another were the arms of the sultan of Aleppo [probably
al-Malik an-Nasir]; in another the arms of the sultan of Babylon [i.e., Cairo;
either al-Kamil Muhammad or as-Salih Ayyub].'

It is known that the half-German, half-Sicilian Emperor Frederick II
(*Stupor mundi*, the wonder of the world) had knighted Fakhr ad-din some
time between the autumn of 1226 and February 1229, but it seems very
curious that both the Emperor and the Ayyubid sultans allowed him to use
an imperial eagle on the chief of his tripartite banner (see below).

Joinville quotes another case where the young prince Bohemund VI of
Antioch was allowed by St.Louis 'to quarter his arms which are scarlet
[correctly, *gules, a bend checky azure and argent*] with the arms of France,
because the king had knighted him' in 1252.

Augmentations or additions to the Arms

These *augmentations* seem to anticipate very closely the system which
showed whether, for example, you supported the successors of Frederick II
or of St. Louis' brother Charles, King of Sicily and Naples, in the battle for
Italy.

The arms of Samminiato on the *disco da parto* (birth tray) which probably
commemorates the birth of a child to Francesco di San Miniato and
Costanza di Bongianni da Gianfigliazzi (married in 1537) are interesting in
that here, as in the Bohemund example, the arms are quartered rather than
placed in chief.

As in the Muslim kingdoms, there was little or no control in Italy over the
adoption of augmentations, or indeed of arms generally. We know that
Frederick II in 1212 granted to Corrado Malaspina the imperial chief to his
arms (*per fesse gules and or, a branch of thorns vert with five flowers argent* –
compare Maltravers, above). Later Emperors permitted their Ghibelline

Pl.VIII Waterpot with the insignia of Qalaun.
Courtesy of Sotheby's London.

Fig.33 An example of the chief of allegiance: the arms of Ottoni, *chequy or and gules, an imperial chief.*

supporters, for instance Visconti and della Scala, to quarter the imperial arms, but many of the families who now pretend to either the *capo* or the *quarto dell'impero* have assumed it without warrant.

The same is true to an even greater extent of their opponents of the Papal or Guelf party, who used the *capo d'Angiò*, but in other Western countries it was the sovereign alone who could grant augmentations.

Charles VI of France in 1394 allowed his cousin Charles d'Albret to quarter the arms of France with his own 'qui sont vermeilles' (that is, plain gules), and five years later the same privilege was granted to the King's brother-in-law, Gian Galeazzo Visconti, Duke of Milan and husband of Isabelle de France.

In 1465 Louis XI, that astute man of business, granted the arms of France to Piero de'Medici, 'having in remembrance the great, praiseworthy and commendable renown acquired by the late Cosmo de'Medici in his deeds and concerns, the which he conducted with so good a virtue and prudence',[25] to be borne on the 'doctor's pill' in centre chief of his arms – *or, six roundles in orle gules*.

The same prudence has been exercised by many of the *noblesse de la banque* who have thus attained 'true nobility'. In the years following the death of the old Queen in 1603 many found it expedient to accept a 'Scottish promise' for a ruined estate and then invest in a Nova Scotia baronetcy!

The Scots *double tressure flory counter-flory* was allowed to some families of royal descent through the female line, but by no means to all. Occasionally, as in the case of Malcolm Fleming, a devoted supporter of Robert Bruce and his son, it was granted to a family not connected by blood to the Royal Line.

Richard II of England (re.1377–99) impaled the fictitious arms of King Edward the Confessor (*azure, a cross patonce between five martlets or*) with his own, and granted it as an augmentation to some of his kinsmen. Among these was Thomas Mowbray, first Duke of Norfolk (d. 1400), the ancestor of Thomas Howard, Lord Surrey, who commanded the English army at the Battle of Flodden in 1513 and was granted by Henry VIII *an escutcheon or, charged with a demi-lion rampant pierced through the mouth by an arrow, within a tressure of Scotland*. His grandson Henry, Earl of Surrey, 'excellent in arts and in arms: a man of learning: a genius and a hero', was executed on 21 January 1547 at the order of the insanely jealous and senile Henry VIII, seemingly for using the full arms and augmentations of his ancestors.

CHAPTER III

THE ISLAMIC HERALDIC SYSTEM AT WORK

During the twelfth century the differences between Christians and Muslims were sometimes difficult to detect, and Usamah can write: 'Behold, the riders were seen advancing in a great mass, preceded by a knight wearing a coat of linked mail and a helmet. He was already close to me; I made for him – and behold! he turned out to be a cavalry commander named Umar.'

Man for man the Christians were usually bigger than the Muslims, and Usamah records that sometimes the Arabs grafted spears together to withstand the charge of the heavier Westerners. He notices a Frankish cavalier 'on a black horse as large as a camel', but he himself owns 'a Frankish coat of mail . . . equipped with the proper linings, felt pads, silk waste and rabbits' hair'.

In the latter part of the century, however, it was the descendants of the Kurdish Ayyub who dominated Egypt and Syria, and it was these lighter armed troops who depended more on the bow and the sword than upon the lance that Westerners associated with 'Saracens' in general.

The greatest of these was al-Malik Salah ad-din, who at the battle of Hattin in 1187 demolished the Christian Kingdom of Jerusalem and very nearly expelled the Westerners from Syria once and for all. The third Crusade brought little real advantage, but when Saladin died in 1193 the country was divided among various branches of the family of Ayyub. One of these was the line of rulers in Hamah who, we have seen, appear consistently to have borne arms *bendy of or, gules, or, sable* (of an indeterminate number), *a chief argent*.

Elsewhere the mamluk Sultans superseded the last of the Ayyubids, and Baybars was able to impose his authority over much of the same area as had Saladin almost a century previously. The line of Hamah received their 'fief' from him, in much the same way as a Western earl or baron received his from an overlord, and may well have added his insignia to their arms.

Fulana, a daughter of Baybars, married another powerful mamluk, al-Mansur Saif ad-din Qalaun, one of whose own daughters was married to Baraka-Khan. After the short reign of Salamish, Qalaun succeeded to the Sultanate as al-Malik al-Mansur in 1280, and founded a dynasty which lasted for 110 years and through five generations.

Insignia of the descendants of Qalaun

It is by studying in some detail the insignia used by him and his descendants that the question of whether the Saracens formulated a true heraldic system can be proved or disproved (see family tree on p.69).

The pottery jar (Plate VIII), '*made for the water of the Maristan* (Hospital) *of an-Nuri'*, is almost certainly unique in portraying the insignia of Qalaun (*argent, a fleur-de-lys gules*). In 1283, having recovered five years before from a serious illness through the good offices of this hospital, he restored the foundation of Nur ad-din Mahmud b. Zangi. Previously the fleur-de-lys depicted here had been tentatively assigned to Nur ad-din, but on the basis of this evidence I think it is more logical to believe that these insignia belonged to the restorer, rather than to the founder.

Therefore we no longer have to rely on the evidence that Saif ad-din Anuk bore *a fleur-de-lys*, the insignia of his grandfather; but can say with some confidence that it was the founder of the dynasty himself who adopted this motif in preference to the lion of Baybars with whom he was connected by marriage.

Of the insignia of his successor Khalil (re.1290–3) we have no definite record, but the latter's brother al-Malik an-Nasir Muhammad used *an eagle* and *six-petalled rosette*.

In the same way that the rule of the powerful Baybars is symbolised by the king of the beasts, that of an-Nasir Muhammad (re.1293–4, 1299–1309 and 1310–41) is portrayed by the lion's aerial counterpart, the eagle – probably *sable and crowned or, on a field argent*. These birds have been found on many works of art and also in the coinage dating from the first two reigns of the Sultan. As in the West, it is depicted in many ways: usually with the wings spread and a single head turned to the left or right, or double headed, crowned or crested, it resembles the German imperial eagle that we have noticed on a chief or quartered with so many Italian families' arms.

We can see from the tree of the Bahri mamluks that the eagle was used by an-Nasir Muhammad's son al-Malik as-Salih (re. 1351–4), his nephew Muzaffar ad-din Musa b. as-Salih Ali (viv. 1288–1318), and his grandson al-Malik al-Mansur b. Hajji (re. 1376–81). It is possible that the eagle was originally adopted not by an-Nasir Muhammad himself but by his elder brother and predecessor al-Malik al-Ashraf Khalil, one of whose amirs, Aqqus al-Ashrafi (d. 1335) bore *eagles*, or perhaps *falcons* (Turkish *aqush* and Persian *aqqus* mean a white bird) on a tray and its support.

An-Nasir's other emblem, the six-petalled rosette, almost certainly *or* on a field *gules*, we have seen before as the royal arms of the Rasulid sultans of Yaman from *c*.1250 to 1441. Qalqashandi says that these were *argent, a five-petalled rosette gules*, and were assumed by al-Malik al-Muzaffar Yusuf when he succeeded the Ayyubid dynasty in this area. Thus it well may be that the Sultans of Egypt and Syria by using a gold field and six-petalled rosette are saying that they are their superiors, who do not recognise the Rasulid authority over the Holy Places.

GENEALOGICAL TABLE: THE QALAUNIDS

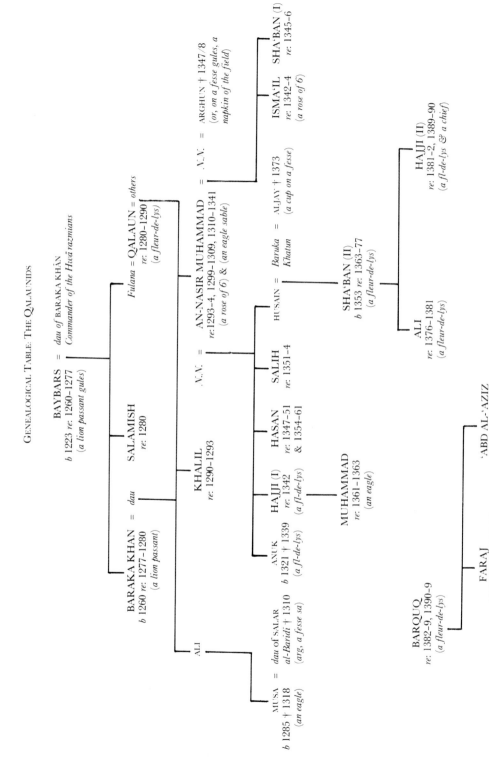

BAYBARS = dau of BARAKA KHĀN
b 1223 re: 1260–1277   Commander of the Hwārazmians
(a lion passant gules)

BARAKA KHAN = dau
b 1260 re: 1277–1280
(a lion passant)

SALAMISH
re: 1280

ALI

KHALIL
re: 1290–1293

Fulana = QALAUN = others
re: 1280–1290
(a fleur-de-lys)

AN-NASIR MUHAMMAD = N.N.
re:1293–4, 1299–1309, 1310–1341
(a rose of 6) & (an eagle sable)

N.N. =

ARGHUN † 1347/8
(or, on a fesse gules, a
napkin of the field)

ISMA'IL
re: 1342–4
(a rose of 6)

SHA'BAN (I)
re: 1345–6

MUSA = dau of SALAR
b 1285 † 1318   al-Baridi † 1310
(an eagle)   (arg, a fesse sa)

ANUK
b 1321 † 1339
(a fl-de-lys)

HAJJI (I)
re: 1342
(a fl-de-lys)

HASAN
re: 1347–51
& 1354–61

SALIH
re: 1351–4

HUSAIN = Baruka
Khatun

ALJAY † 1373
(a cup on a fesse)

MUHAMMAD
re: 1361–1363
(an eagle)

SHA'BAN (II)
b 1353 re: 1363–77
(a fleur-de-lys)

BARQUQ
re: 1382–9, 1390–9
(a fleur-de-lys)

FARAJ
re: 1399–1405, 1406–12
(a fleur-de-lys)

'ABD AL-'AZIZ
re: 1405–1406
(an inscribed cartouche)

ALI
re: 1376–1381
(a fleur-de-lys)

HAJJI (II)
re: 1381–2, 1389–90
(a fl-de-lys & a chief)

From S. Lane-Poole, *The Mohammadan Dynasties* (1925), and E. de Zambaur, *Manuel* (1927).
Reproduced from the *Palestine Exploration Quarterly*, 1982 1.

The fleur-de-lys, the eagle and the rosette.

Three main charges therefore seem to have been used from the early years of the dynasty of Qalaun: the fleur-de-lys, the eagle and the rosette. Of these the rosette (perhaps copied from the Rasulids) seems to have been the dynastic arms, while the other two were family insignia. The eagle appears during four reigns and the fleur-de-lys in at least five, culminating in the shield *party per fesse, a fleur-de-lys in base* of al-Malik as-Salih Hajji (re.1381–2 and 1389–90).

It is interesting to note that the first two sultans of the Burji group (men of the fort), al-Malik az-Zahir Barquq and his elder son Faraj, perhaps in a conscious effort to provide a sense of continuity for their amirs and less important illiterate subjects, adopted the plain fleur-de-lys. The double headed eagle of the Holy Roman Empire was of course used by successive dynasties in preference to their paternal arms.

Like the lion of Baybars, these three charges were used as liveries by amirs and other court officials: it is odd perhaps that Abu'l-Fida' of Hamah did not copy his cousin al-Muzaffar and place one of them upon his chief when he was granted the sultanate by Qalaun.

A fleur-de-lys on a bipartite shield was used by Najm ad-din Mahmud (*argent, a fleur-de-lys and a chief gules*), as we have seen, and by Haidar Ibn al-Askari (*c*.1382); examples on tripartite ones seem to centre around Saif ad-din Aynab, a mamluk of Barquq and *jamdar* to his son Faraj, who reigned from 1453–61 as al-Malik al-Ashraf and bore *a penbox, a cup and a fleur-de-lys* (see below).

Examples of rosettes are rare, but on the ceiling of the Vestibule of the Mausoleum in Cairo appear the arms of Abu Muhammad Mahmud b. Ahmad al-Aini al-Qadi, who was born in 1361, was chief of police in 1399, and died in 1451; they are *per fesse, gules, a penbox argent, and dark brown (tenné?), a vase or, between two six-petalled rosettes argent*. On the mausoleum of the amir Bahadur-as as-silahdar a rosette has been replaced by a pair of swords, and on a public fountain in Aleppo are the arms of Baybugha al-Qasimi (exec.1353), *on a fesse a cup between two six-petalled rosettes*.

Objects also survive which include an eagle and insignia of office; for example, in the British Museum are two mosque lamps of Tuquztamur al-Hamawi (d. 1345) which bear *gules, a cup surmounted by an eagle or, a chief plain*; Bahadur al-Hamawi, chief Master of the Robes to an-Nasir Muhammad, bore *a napkin surmounted by an eagle on a plain field*; and some tripartite shields have an eagle in chief and a napkin in fesse.

The arms attributed to Fakhr ad-din by Joinville in 1250 have an eagle in chief and two other divisions. Again, the French historian seems to be noting developments in Islamic insignia much too early – in this case, nearly 140 years too soon, for the earliest tripartite blazon that I know is that of Sharaf ad-din Yunus an-Nauruzi (d. 1389), who bore *1. a penbox, 2. a cup, 3. a cup*. He was a mamluk of Jurji an-Nauruzi, *dawadar* to Sultan Barquq (re.1382–9 and 1390–8), and *grand-dawadar* in 1382.

Second stage of amiral insignia

It was during the long reign of an-Nasir Muhammad (or perhaps more exactly during the gap between his first and second periods of rule, in 1294–9) that the developments leading to the second stage of amiral insignia took place. It was no longer common practice, except for members of the sultanic family itself, to bear single charges on a plain field.

Zain ad-din Kitbugha b. Abdallah al-Mansuri, who was alive in 1253, bore in his early life *a cup*, but when he became Sultan as al-Malik al-Adil in 1294 he was bearing *or, a fesse and a cup in base gules*, which were inherited by his son Nasir ad-din Muhammad. His sultanic banners were yellow, as were those of the unnamed Sultan (presumably as-Salih Ayyub, or, less likely, his son Taran Shah) whom Joinville saw in 1249–50. If he is right, the beginnings of the change from single charges to bipartite shields together with a formalised system of amiral arms based on those of the Sultan must be dated to the middle of the thirteenth century, and this would agree well with the testimony of Abu'l-Mahasin already referred to.

What is certain is that by the end of the century bipartite shields with the cup of the *saqi* as the main charge are by far the most common. Three other official blazons, those of the *silahdar*, the *jamdar*, and the *dawadar*, come next, with a number of shields charged with a *plain fesse* or a number of *bars*. Mayer regards this as the emblem of the *baridi* (despatch rider), because three important amirs, Saif ad-din Salar (d. 1310), the father-in-law of an-Nasir Muhammad's nephew Musa, and Ala'ad-din Sanjar al-Jawli (d. 1345) bore *argent, a fesse sable*, and another with the same title, Ala'ad-din Ali al-Baridi, also bore *a fesse*. It is not clear whether this fesse symbolises the straight road of the royal post officers or the royal inscribed insignia that they carried. Indeed, because five other equally important amirs who were not apparently despatch riders (that is, Lajin, Kujkhun and another Saif ad-din Arghun the *dawadar*, Saif ad-din Baktamur and his son Jamal ad-din Ibrahim) also bore a plain fesse, it may merely mark a stage between bipartite and charged tripartite shields.

The lion, the eagle and the rosette begin to die out, and of non-official

Fig.34 Mosque lamp showing tripartite inscription on a roundle of Barquq (*re.* 1382–98).

charges the fleur-de-lys alone remains in any number. The strange *horse with a ceremonial saddle* appears once, on a facsimile lamp in the British Museum, the field argent and the fesse gules. These are the arms of Ala'ad-din Ali b. Baktamur, the brother of Ibrahim just mentioned, and this small family group provides the only instance where a father and son used the same arms and a brother (presumably younger) differenced the paternal arms.

It was at this time that Sultanic practice and that of the amirs, nearly always bearing by now insignia of office, took quite different paths.

The Sultanic inscribed cartouche

An-Nasir Muhammad in his third reign instituted the custom of using a shield or more exactly a cartouche from which all the charges were deleted and replaced by mottoes in praise of the ruling Sultan. The first types had a phrase in the middle part of a tripartite cartouche, but later the inscriptions were increased in length and eventually filled all three portions. Many of the mottoes start 'izz li-mawlana' (glory to our lord), followed by the Sultan's name, titles and the name of his father, and end 'khallada Allah mulkahu' (may God perpetuate his kingdom). From its introduction until the very end of the Burji period, this form of cartouche was used by all the Sultans without exception, though the dynastic and family insignia did not completely die out.

As each Sultan's motto was an individual one and therefore could not be inherited, it is impossible to call this system an heraldic one. If, however, the cartouches were carried to war in the same way as we know they were worn round the necks of the Sultan's subjects, they would still qualify as Armorial Insignia. However, it seems more likely that the Qalaunid insignia were used armorially and the inscribed cartouche was the Sultan's personal badge used as a livery by his courtiers.

There is a comparable but not identical development to this system in two Western countries. As early as the twelfth century's end we find in the little-known Provençal *Chanson de geste Roland at Saragossa* (lines 133–4), where Oliver is being armed,

> Pueys li aportan .i. escut de cartier,
> non hi ac penchura, mas amb aur fon letretz.

> Then they bring him a quartered shield,
> No painting, but gold letters on its field.

In Italy the well-known arms of Rome, *gules, in bend a Latin cross and the letters SPQR* (Senatus Populus-Que Romanus) *or*, and those of the noble family of d'Avanzo, where the initials UAPD appear on a bend sinister (*Usque Ad Postremum Diem*, which equals roughly 'faithful unto death'), provide two examples. In Spain too, where the custom is very wide-spread, the civic arms of Cadiz, Malaga and San Sebastian all have wide borders inscribed with pious mottoes. It is perhaps no coincidence that Italy, with its close trading links with Islam, and Spain, where the Nasrids ruled in Granada until 1492, are the two countries where this convention is most prominent.

Having studied the Sultanic insignia, we come to the conclusion that contact during the Crusades with the developing heraldry of the Western knights may have influenced the Ayyubids of Hamah, the son of Baybars, the Qalaunids and some of the Bahri Mamluks to adopt hereditary insignia. However, the introduction of inscribed Sultanic cartouches halted this trend, and after the death of Faraj in 1412 royal proto-heraldry and indeed the use of royal Armorial Insignia came to an abrupt end.

Third stage of amiral insignia

The third stage in the development of amiral insignia starts around 1325 and continues up till the sultanate of Qa'itbay (1468–95); the number of charges decreases once more and a difference begins to appear between the 'men of the pen' (*arbab al-aqlam*) and the 'men of the sword' (*arbab as-suyuf*), who were 'the mamluks of the Sultan' (*mamalik sultaniyya*). The 'men of the pen' were either free-born Arabs or the sons of mamluks, and both these groups were ineligible for a military career, so they had to join the bureaucratic side of government. A penbox was their principal charge; it appears most usually in chief, frequently in fesse, but very seldom in base.

Muhibb ad-din, whose copper dish marked with his blazon of *a penbox between two napkins on a three-fielded shield* is in the Victoria and Albert Museum, was a scribe in the Treasury of Damascus and almost certainly belonged to the professional scribal class. The long-lived Saif ad-din Qanibay, who died in 1462 aged eighty, was not a member of this group. He started his career as a mamluk and was made an amir in 1438; his insignia epitomise the vulgarity of some of the blazons of this period, for no colour sense or balance of design seems to have been applied; it is: *1. gules, a scimitar azure; 2. or, a penbox argent; 3. vert, a cup gules between two horns argent, ends or.* By contrast the arms of Saif ad-din Tashtamur al-Ala'i, the *grand-dawadar* of al-Malik al-Kamil Sha'ban (*sanguine, on a fesse or a penbox sable*), who died in 1384, are very pleasing.

Fig.35 Roundle of Muhibb ad-din from a
coppered dish.

The sword and the fleur-de-lys are by now almost defunct (except in the
arms of the group of amirs connected with al-Malik al-Ashraf, re. 1453–61).
He was originally the mamluk of al-Malik az-Zahir Barquq (d.1399) and
became *jamdar* to his son, al-Malik an-Nasir Faraj (d. 1412); both of them
bore *a fleur-de-lys*. His name too indicates his allegiance to these two sultans,

for he is called Saif ad-din Aynal b. Abdallah az-Zahiri an-Nasiri (literally, Aynal, the son of no-one, the man of Barquq and of Faraj). A minaret in Gaza bears his blazon: *1. a penbox 2. a cup 3. a fleur-de-lys*, which was inherited by his amir and marshal, Barsbay al-Ashrafi (d. 1473), and differenced by Saif ad-din Timraz, his amir, *jamdar* and *saqi* (d. 1497): *1. a diapered penbox 2. a diapered cup charged with a napkin between two horns 3. a diapered fleur-de-lys*.

The napkin holds its place, but by far the most popular charge is the cup. This was borne either in base or, more usually, in fesse, where in several cases it is charged with two smaller cups; in chief it appears only when the blazon is *three cups in pale* (one in each division).

Dr Meinecke argues most convincingly, using such evidence as I have demonstrated for the fleur-de-lys, that the arrangement of charges on tripartite shields is determined by the arms of successive cupbearers who became sultans and influenced the combination of charges adopted by the amirs created during their reigns.

It is at this time that the *pair of horns* first appears; in my opinion they are the visible sign that a mamluk has been made an amir, for Qalqashandi said that 'the investiture of an amir included the presentation to him of a horn and flag'. Towards the end of the Burji period (in the late fifteenth century) a corporate insignia had been formulated for the warrior class, which is generally known as a *Qa'itbay blazon*, after the Sultan under whom it may well have originated. As too few of these blazons survive in colour, it is not possible to judge whether each amir used a distinctive chromatic scheme. However, this seems very probable, for, though there were never more than a few thousand amirs at any one time, there are more than 13 million possible variations of the design, using the two metals and five heraldic tinctures!

Though the rather surrealist portrayal of the interior of a penbox may at first be difficult to identify, and the horse with a sacred saddle be unfamiliar, the majority of Islamic charges would be quite acceptable in Western Heraldry. Some of the tripartite shields are not very beautiful, but they are no worse than a great deal of sixteenth-century European coats of arms; the 'Qa'itbay blazons' particularly are very good pieces of design.

Tamgas and tribal signs

However, throughout the whole period under discussion, that is, from the end of the twelfth century to the introduction of a corporate amiral blazon in the second half of the fifteenth, we find a small number of charges which are quite unlike anything used in Western Europe. These are the *tamgas*, which, I believe, are first mentioned, and completely misunderstood, by Western writers of the early *Chansons de geste*. In the *Roland*, of *c.*1100, which is the first of the genre that survives, we have the description of an amiral banner or *dragon*:

> Li amiralz mult par est riches hoem
> dedavant sei fait porter sun dragon
> e l'estandart Terragan e Mahum
> E un'ymagen Apolin le felun.

> This amir was a mighty man and strong
> before him was displayed his own dragon
> with Termagent and Mahmoud painted on
> and th'image of their devil Apollon.

In the *Chanson des Chétifs*, written later in the same century, we have these lines about another of the many shields of Cornumarans:

> A son col pent la targe qui fu a eschequier
> .i. escharbocle i ot en la bocle a or mier
> Mahomes estoit pains el senestre quartier
> et le bon arc Turcois ne volt il pas laissier

> Around his neck a chequered shield he wears
> with boss and buckle made of gold most rare
> from the left quarter the face of Mahoun stares
> and by his side his trusty Turkish bow he bears

And thirdly, a sustained piece from the *Chanson de Jérusalem*, which seems to have influenced the author of the late thirteenth-century *Galiens li Restorés*, where the figure of the Prophet on a banner 'holds a Christian and beats him with a sword':

> Onques nus hom de char ne vit si haut clochier
> Lassus siet Apollins, en sa main .i. sautier
> Où la lois est escrite dès Adan le premier
> Sovent le fait li vens la amont torniier
> .i. baston en sa main, por franchois manechier.
> Semblant fait à son doit de la enseignier
> Par l'art de yngremanche li font dire et nonchier
> Que tot crestien doivent a Sodant aplochier.

> Out of the cart it rose high as a church spire,

On it was Apollin with his psaltire
Where all the law from Adam was writ clear,
And in the wind it turned from here to there.
A staff he had which caused the Franks to fear
As giver of the law this rod he would not spare –
Black magic made him move and loud declare
That every Christian now the Sultan must revere.

These are by no means isolated examples, yet it is plainly impossible that the figure of an instructor in the Law, or indeed any other human shape – be it Apollyon, Termagant, or the Prophet himself – could be portrayed on a banner of the orthodox Sunni armies of the Ayyubids.

The description in Ambroise (c.1191–6) of Negro troops with red head-dresses at Acre who 'each had a banner with Mahumet portrayed at the top' reminds one of Joinville's account of Barbaquam (Baraka Khan, the father-in-law of Baybars) and his 'three hundred men, who were Khorasmuns [Hwarazmians] . . . They carried red banners, with indentations right up the shafts of their lances, at the tip of which they had fixed heads made out of hair, that looked like the heads of devils.'

These last seem to be accurate, and I believe that Ambroise's *enseigne Mahumet / Qui estoit portraite en somet* and Joinville's *heads of hair that looked like devils* may provide the answer. One need not question the eyesight of Western chroniclers; what they saw did look to them like pictures of devils – in the case of Apollin, seeming to point at a Muslim text. What is at fault is their critical faculty, conditioned by their views of Islam and the East in general that Muslims were idol-worshippers and nigromancers who might, by craft or magic, have produced automata to direct their troops. Or they might have thought, by analogy with their own customs, that these heathen were following the banner of their 'patron saint'.

My hypothetical reconstruction of an inscribed amiral banner may well be 'the instructor of the Law' or the 'image of Mahomet' that Christian commentators actually saw. Of the twenty-four *tamgas* of the Oghuz Turkish tribes, known from the Leiden University manuscript, some, with prejudiced eyes, could be seen as representations of the human figure; the bifurcated 'sword of the Prophet' has also the approximate shape of a man with outstretched arms.

Shaikh Ilyas b. Sabiq b. Khidr (d. 1272) and Nur ad-din Ali b. Shihab ad-din Bishara (d. 1295), the great amir, both used the blazon that I have illustrated. This is Dr Mayer's Emblem 24, which may well correspond with *tamgas* 10, 12 and 18 in the Leiden MS.

Fig.36 Artist's impressions of an amiral banner bearing a *tamga* and another decorated with the bifurcated 'sword of the Prophet'.

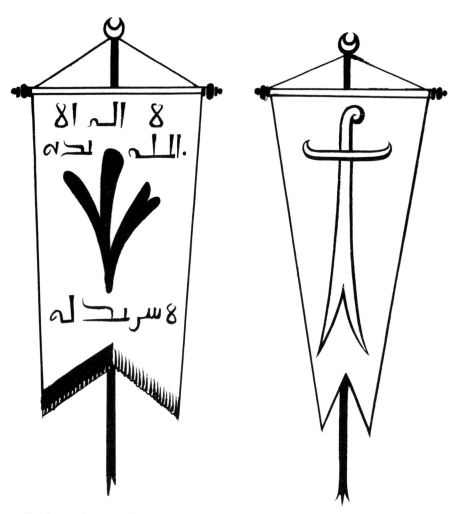

In the early period Muhammad al-Alawi bore Emblem 33 (? *tamgas* 1, 7, 11 and 24), Sungur as-Sadi the inspector of the army (d. 1328) Emblem 41 (*tamgas* 4 and 8), the amir Salah ad-din b. Samri Emblem 43 (*tamgas* 6, 14, 17 and 23), and the amir Muhammad b. Ahmad b. Timur al Ala'i Emblem 8, which may possibly be another form of Emblem 26.

This latter is borne once in the first, twice in the second and once on blazons of the third period (by Saif ad-din Ulmas, mamluk of an-Nasir Muhammad, his taster in 1317, who was executed in *c.*1333 [*argent, Emblem 26 or*]). The field is creamy white, as are the field and chief of the insignia of Shihab ad-din (Ahmad) b. Saif ad-din Faragi, amir of an-Nasir (*argent, Emblem 26 gules, a chief of the first*).

Ghars ad-din Khatil's uncoloured blazon has a targe or table-top charged with Emblem 26, on a fesse, and finally Jamal ad-din Yusuf b. Ahmad, the

Fig.37 Table of emblems and *tamgas*: on the *left*, *tamgas* from the Leiden manuscript, and, *right*, possible equivalents, from Mayer's *Saracenic Heraldry*.

Pl.IX Two so-called Qaitbay roundles, one from the picture in the Louvre showing the 'Meeting with the Venetian Ambassadors'; the other, using gold, black and silver, shows the insignia of the Viceroy of Syria, Barquq (*d.*1473).

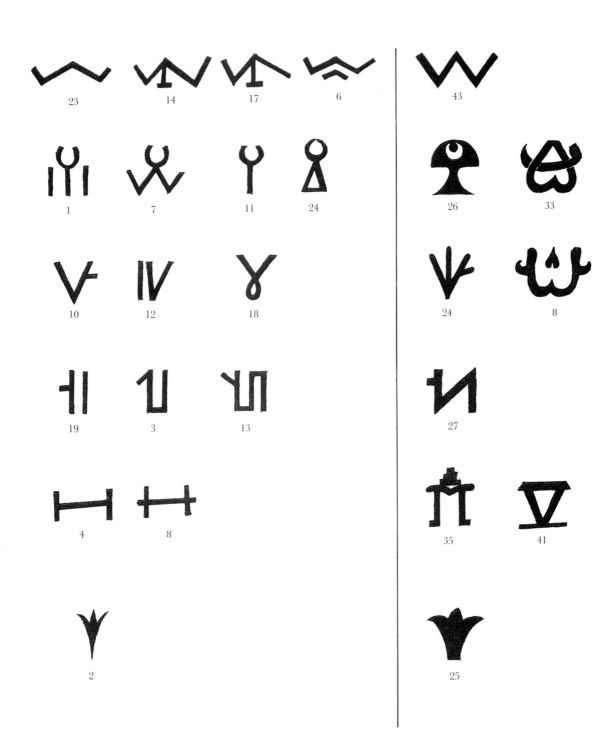

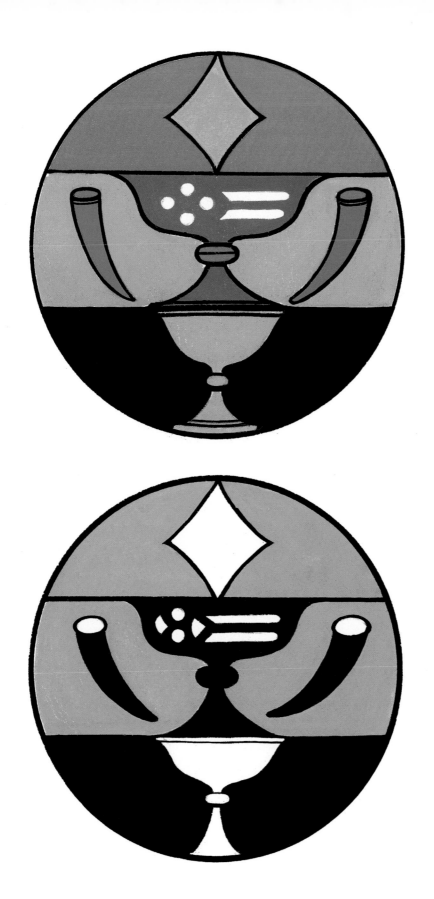

Pl.X A Venetian dish with the arms of a Medici pope, either Leo X (1513–21) or Clement VII (1523–34), surmounted by the tiara and the keys of St Peter (*dexter azure, sinister or*). Notice the roundle in the centre chief representing the augmentation of France.

keeper of the privy purse, who was executed in 1467, bore a tripartite shield *1. a penbox 2. a scimitar with bands 3. Emblem 26.*

Pieces of enamelled glass, the remains of a beaker of *c*.1250–60, have recently been found, during rebuilding, in Lombard Street, Abingdon. Two of these fragments contain unmistakable roundles *gules, Emblem 26 argent*, which with another (unfortunately destroyed) and a pious inscription to the Sultan formed a frieze around the neck of the drinking cup. They are displayed in Abingdon Museum.

Another of an-Nasir's amirs was Ala'ad-din Ali b. Fakhr ad-din Isa at-Turkumani, whose insignia, included in a foundation text on a public fountain in Cairo by his widow Salma, were *on a fesse Emblem 27* (*tamgas* 3, 13 and 19). The epithet 'at-Turkumani' puts the *tamga* in its correct setting, for the Turkomans originated on the upland plains to the West of Afghanistan. Here the horses of the rulers of Bactria were famous throughout the ancient world; tribal names of dependants of the royal house of Kavanida included Zariaspai, 'golden horses' and Arimaspai, 'well-schooled horses'. Bactrian lancers fought for the Achaemenids, and Alexander the Great remounted many of his cavalrymen on horses from these fertile and healthy uplands, and used in his Far Eastern campaigns Bactrian mercenaries.

With the break-up of the empire of Alexander, Bactria became again an independent kingdom, Hellenistic in culture, with contacts with the Far East. In 126 BC envoys of the Chinese Emperor reported that 'in the distant land of Taiynan (Bactrian Ferghana) marvellous blood-sweating heavenly horses are bred'.

Marco Polo wrote: 'They breed a great many excellent horses, very swift . . . in the province of Badasan (North Afghanistan) there was until recently a breed of horses that were descended from Bucephalus, Alexander the Great's horse, and among them the foals were born with *a star and a crescent moon* on their foreheads, as if Bucephalus himself had covered the mare . . .'

In 1850 A. Boru, a traveller to Bokhara, reported: 'I observed something I would not have believed credible – that the neck arteries of Turkoman horses did in fact exude blood after severe exhaustion or when they were heated.'

One can see the 'star and crescent moon of Bucephalus' among the signs that decorated the high hats of the Sassanian nobility, and find an almost infinite number of its variations carved on rocks and in caves throughout the Near East. The simplicity of these marks, whether tribal or personal, made them ideal as brand-marks for the stock of the semi-nomadic herdsmen. One hears of them also on banners, as when the great standard of Kawa 'made the world look yellow, red and violet'; in the *Shahnamah*, Bijen, the son of

Guiv, had a flag 'decorated with a figure of the moon, on a purple background with black fringes', another with 'a shining figure of the sun', and others with 'animals and stars'.

Perhaps we hear of them again at the beginning of the twelfth century, when '. . . everything was placed in front of his tent, even down to coverlets and saddlebags. Then Salahdin seated himself, whilst we formed a circle round, and invited those who could recognise their property to swear to it, and to take their goods away.'[26]

However 'Islamicised' the mamluks became, there seem to have been at all periods some who did not forget their origins in the horse-raising lands of South East Asia, and it was the insignia of these few that had the most influence on other heraldic systems; the cup, the napkin, the sword and the penbox may well be the origins of the four suits of our modern playing-cards, but the *tamgas* have dominated the heraldry of Eastern Europe for nearly five hundred years.

Reasons for the failure of Islamic 'heraldry'

At the outset of the Mamluk period there seems to have been in force an idea of hereditary rule, and thus the Qalaunids, though in many cases not effective Sultans, reigned for over a century and initiated a proto-heraldic system of inherited insignia. However, the adoption of the inscribed cartouche by an-Nasir Muhammad (see figure 34), despite the re-introduction of the fleur-de-lys by the Burji Sultans Barquq and his son Faraj, meant the total disappearance of Sultanic Heraldry.

Likewise, though the dynastic principle, particularly by adoption, may have influenced the insignia of the amirs, these were men of the first generation, freed slaves, rising through toughness and ability, and eligible to become the leaders of their society. They were self-made soldier-statesmen, intensely proud of their caste, whose sons, in most cases, were debarred from the paths their fathers had trodden. Thus there was no true hereditary principle and no real pride in descent, which is essential to the development of Armory as we understand it in the West, and so, before the Ottoman gunfire wiped out this society, its Heraldry had already become sterile.

'Nothing but firearms caused harm to the Circassians . . . God curse the man who invented them, and curse the man who fires on Muslims with them'; the captured Sultan Tumanbay said to the Ottoman Sultan Selim, 'We are Muslims and why do you consider lawful the killing of Muslims, and how can you fire on them with cannon and firearms? What would you do if you stood in the presence of God, and what would you answer?'[27]

CHAPTER IV

PARALLELS IN WESTERN HERALDRY

As we have seen, the fleur-de-lys was called by Muslims the *faransisiya* (the emblem of the Franks), and this would argue a French, or perhaps more likely a Venetian, origin. The fleur-de-lys is found in both these areas before true heraldry developed and was adopted as an heraldic charge very early in the twelfth century.

Dr Mayer, however, sees two distinct forms: in the West one where the fleurons grow from one stem, in the East a flower of three elements bound together by a band, and argues that it was from this latter that the heraldic *fleur-de-lys* or *fleur-de-glaieul* (*gladiolus*, little sword) developed. I am not, however, convinced of this, and consider it more likely that this decorative charge was introduced into the Near East by Venetian merchants rather than *vice versa*.

The earliest examples we have are in Syria, on two buildings, a madrasa in Damascus, and the main mosque in Hims, which are closely associated with Nur ad-din Mahmud b. Zangi, ruler of this area from 1146–73 (see above).

If these blazons are really contemporary with the buildings, we could extend the origin of Islamic heraldic insignia back to about 1154, that is, to within three years of the funeral plaque of Geoffrey, Count of Anjou. This would make the developments noted by Joinville more likely to have taken place as early as 1249, for within a hundred years a development from single charge to more complicated blazon would surely have gained impetus.

We have noticed the inscriptional elements of some Italian and Iberian shields, and have looked quite closely at the ancient *tamgas*, the origin of many of the strange devices found in Balkan and Polish heraldry.

The cup, the napkin, the sword and the penbox, the commonest of mamluk charges (as well as being the possible basis of the four suits of cards) appear, sometimes in the same form, sometimes not, in European heraldry.

The penbox has no equivalent in Western armory, but the *quill* or *ostrich feather* is famous from the 'shield of peace' of Edward Plantagenet, the Black Prince: *sable, three ostrich feathers quilled argent and passing through scrolls of the same, bearing the words ICH DIEN*. Woodward (p.592ff.) and the editors of *Boutell's Heraldry* (pp.164ff.) refute the legend that these feathers were won from the blind King John of Bohemia at Crecy, and suggest that they may have been introduced into England by Edward's mother Philippa of Hainault – where they were connected with the county of Ostrevant. Several members of the Plantagenet dynasty used them as badges; as well as the 'arms of Edward the Confessor', Thomas Duke of Norfolk was granted them by Richard II. His rival Henry Bolingbroke, afterwards Henry IV, used *a feather enfiled with a garter, bearing the word SOVEREYGNE*, and this

Fig.38 Prince of Wales' feathers on a
background of his livery colours, murrey and
blue.

motto may well be the origin of the 'Collar of SS' found on the effigies of so many supporters of the House of Lancaster.[28] However, feathers were used too by the Yorkists, and it was not until the reign of the Tudor Henry VII that they were reserved exclusively for the Prince of Wales.

They were used as charges by John Chaundeler, Bishop of Salisbury (1417–26), and among others as canting arms by the family of Cowpen of Oxford: *gules, six writing-pens, three, two and one argent*. It seems a very appropriate charge for the *noblesse de la robe*, and as we know the pen is mightier than the sword. As crest, a *panache* or *cluster of ostrich feathers*, often coloured alternately in the tinctures of the shield, was used widely throughout Europe in the early period of Heraldry, when crests were largely limited to the higher nobility; peacock feathers were also used, but these because of their fine appearance were normally *proper*. In modern European heraldry it is still the practice, where no crest has been granted, to place a panache above the helm. German arms often have two buffelhorns coloured as the arms, sometimes alone, sometimes either side of the crest, and in some cases decorated with flags or feathers.

The English family of Profumo, for instance, who were barons of Sardinia and of the United Kingdom of Italy, bear *gules, a fesse argent, in chief a chaplet of laurel proper; the shield surmounted by an Italian Baron's coronet proper*; in this case *a panache of five gules, argent, vert, argent, gules, issuant from the coronet* could be added.

The napkin we have already seen as a *lozenge* and discussed its uses, and as these bear no resemblance to the duties of the Master of the Robes we will go on to the sword.

This martial charge is borne by many families, including Spada of Rome; *gules, three swords in bend sinister, points downwards, argent, garnished or, a chief of France*; and *azure, a sword argent* is the arms of Ferri, of Genoa. It is nearly always borne in its natural colours, but its main interest in this context is as a symbol of office.

The Electors, and subsequently kings, of Saxony, Arch-Marshals of the Empire, bore *per fesse sable and argent, two swords in saltire gules*. The earls of Erroll, Great Constables of Scotland, bear *argent, three escutcheons gules*, behind the shield set *in saltire two batons argent tipped or*, accompanied by their offical badge, *two arms vambraced, issuing out of clouds and gauntleted proper, each holding a sword erect in pale argent, hilted and pommelled or*. The Dukes of Norfolk, Earls Marshal and Hereditary Marshals of England, have behind their arms *two gold batons, in saltire, enamelled at the ends sable*.

The office of hereditary King's Champion seems to have been held by the family of Marmion for the lordships of Scrivelsby and Tamworth – that is,

Fig.39 Bottle dated 1712 of Augustus the Strong, showing the arms of the Arch-marshalship.

Fig.40 Detail from an early 17th-century jug of the Duke of Saxony with his shield of office.

by the service of appearing armed in the royal arms, on the King's best charger, to make proof for the King against any who opposed his coronation. Sir Philip Marmion seems to have held his manors in this way, and it has been argued that he acquired them through marriage with Joan, the heiress of Hugh de Kilpek, because to this family has been attributed arms *argent, a sword in bend sable* (though this is not found in any mediaeval roll of arms).

The accompanying family tree shows how the office descended, not without difficulty, to the Dymokes, who continue to fulfil this obligation for the manor of Scrivelsby (and who bear the *canting motto PRO REGE DIMICO*, I fight for the King).

On the tree is the name of Ralph le Boteler, and his family too have a

87

personal coat and an official one, which can be compared with those of the *silahdar* or the *saqi*: their arms, *or, a chief indented azure*, they quarter with the official coat, *gules, three covered cups or*.

Though these are isolated examples, a practice which is closer to mamluk usage does exist in the West. This is the granting of arms to Guild Companies, which started in the last years of the fourteenth century and still continues. The accompanying examples show the use of tradesmen's tools, scientific instruments, articles of clothing, and food and drink, in heraldry of this kind.

Art historians will, I think, agree that Hispano-Moresque Manises work forms a link between Islamic ceramics and later Italian *majolica*. This can perhaps be heraldically illustrated by the Iznik plate (acc. no. EFC 324) in the Ashmolean, made for the Western market and decorated with arms on an oval cartouche (*per bend argent and azure, a bend gules between two eight-pointed stars counterchanged*); the Nasrid tiles from the Alhambra, at Granada; and the shield of the d'Avanzo family, mentioned above.

Iberian Heraldry

The inscribed cartouche of an-Nasir Muhammad and his successors is a good example of how much importance was attached to the exact word. The religious education of Jews and Muslims is very firmly based on the learning by heart of sacred texts, and it was in areas of the West where Semitic culture was particularly strong that it is possible to see some traces of this in heraldry.

Heraldry that is essentially of Spain and Portugal can often be recognised by the use of bordures either charged or inscribed. The family of Valdivia bears *on a bordure gules the motto LA MUERTE MENOS TEMIDA DA MÁS VIDA* (the less death is feared, the more it confers life); that of Villa has around its first quarter *UN BUEN MORIRE DE LA VIDA ES GLORIA* (a good death is life's glory); and in the Museum is a tile charged with the arms of Mendoza: *Quarterly per saltire 1 & 4: vert, a bend gules fimbriated or* (bordered with a narrow gold band); *2 & 3: or, AVE MARIA GRATIA PLENA in orle azure*. Bordures semy of charges are also used to show alliance with or political allegiance to more important families: for instance, the family of Cueva, Dukes of Albuquerque, record the marriage of Beltran, the first Duke, with Mencia Mendoza, a daughter of the Duke of Infantado, by placing around their arms *a bordure gules charged with alternately seven saltires and as many escutcheons of Mendoza*.

Another, more familiar, example of this appears in the royal arms of Portugal, which are surrounded by *a bordure of Castile*, to indicate alliances

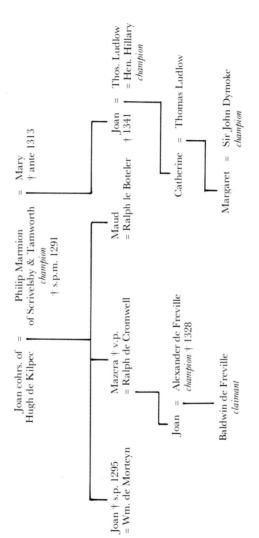

Joan cohrs. of = Philip Marmion = Mary
Hugh de Kilpec of Scrivelsby & Tamworth † ante 1313
champion
† s.p.m. 1291

Joan † s.p. 1295
= Wm. de Morteyn

Mazera † v.p.
= Ralph de Cromwell

Maud
= Ralph le Boteler

Joan
† 1341
= Thos. Ludlow
= Hen. Hillary
champion

Joan = Alexander de Freville
champion † 1328

Baldwin de Freville
claimant

Catherine = Thomas Ludlow

Margaret = Sir John Dymoke
champion

Arms of Marmion: *Vair, a fesse gules paillé* (a form of *diapering,* q.v.)
for the King's Champion: *Sable, a sword, point in chief, argent.*
Arms of Dymoke: *Sable, two lions passant argent.*
for the King's Champion: *Argent, a sword, point in chief, sable.*

89

Fig.42 A tile showing the arms of the
Apothecaries' Company: *Azure, Apollo, the
inventor of physic, proper, his head radiant, holding in
his left hand a bow and in his right an arrow,
supplanting a serpent argent.*

Fig.43 Detail of a sword stand showing the arms
of the Company of Plaisterers, which are typical
of those granted during the reign of Henry VIII
and make for very muddled heraldry.

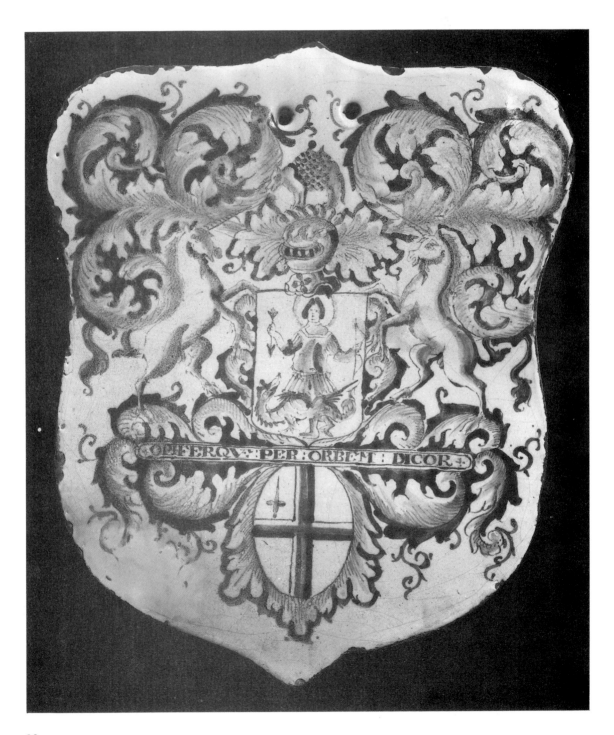

Fig.44 A 15th-century Iznik plate decorated
with Western arms which do not exactly match
any particular family. *Courtesy of the Ashmolean
Museum*

between the two houses. It is interesting that the arms of the Borja Pope, Calixtus III, were *or, a bull passant gules grazing on a terrace vert, a bordure of the first charged with eight tufts of grass of the third*; here the division between field and bordure is indicated only by a line.

The bordure compony, as we have seen, often indicates an illegitimate ancestor (see Plate IV), though this has not always been the case. The system of cadency marks is a comparatively modern one, and at different periods different *brisures* have been used. The present family of Talbot, the premier Earls of Shrewsbury, bear *gules, a lion rampant and a bordure engrailed or*; and we have an example on the hatchment above of the later spurious Montagus, bearing the Montacute arms *argent, three fusils conjoined in fesse gules* within *a bordure sable*.

Fig.45 Nasrid tile from the Hall of Justice in the Alhambra, made in Malaga in the 14th century. The inscription on the bend reads: 'Glory to our Lord and his victory'.

Fig.46 Quartered arms on a square cartouche of
the family of Buyl, lords of Manises, near
Valencia. Glazed ware of the 2nd half of the
15th century.

Fig.47 Tile with the Mendoza arms quarterly
per saltire.

John of Eltham, the second son of Edward II, bore *England, a bordure of France*, and the fighting bishop Henry Le Despencer of Norwich (1370–1406) differenced his arms with *a bordure semy of mitres*. At present the Court of the Lord Lyon operates a system of bordures to difference cadets of the same family: for instance, Campbell of Possil bears *gyronny of eight or and sable, in chief a molet counterchanged, a bordure indented azure charged with eight buckles of the first*, and a cadet of Underriver House has the bordure *embattled vert charged with eight buckles or*.

Heraldry in Italy

The arms of Florence – *argent, a fleur-de-lys fleuretty gules* (formerly with the tinctures reversed) – are one of the most beautiful in the world, and it would therefore be appropriate if it was from Italian merchants that Islam borrowed this charge.

The arms of many other Italian cities are of pure simple design and contrast very favourably with the Civic Heraldry of some other European countries. Bari (*per pale argent and gules*), Ferrara (*per fesse sable and argent*), Messina (*gules, a cross or*) and Siena (*per fesse argent and sable*) are outstanding examples.

Italian families, however, because of the political confusion endemic to this country, often bear numerous augmentations from France (Anjou-Sicile), the Empire or the Papacy. D. Galbreath[29] explains the arms of Este: 1. The Empire (*or, an eagle sable*) for the Vicariate granted to Borso d'Este with the county of Rovigo (see 4) by Frederick III in 1452; 2 & 3. France differenced (*azure, three fleurs-de-lys or, a bordure indented compony gules and argent*), granted to Niccolò, marchese d'Este, by Charles VII in 1431/2; 4. Rovigo (*per pale azure and or, a two-headed eagle per pale argent and sable*); for the Duchy of Ferrara and the papal Gonfaloniership, *on a pale gules the Keys of St.Peter surmounted by a Papal tiara*, and over all Este (*azure, an eagle argent*).

Ecclesiastical Arms

For the origins of Papal and ecclesiastical heraldry we must once again look back to the Bayeux Tapestry; in plates 50–51, 53 and 68–69 of the Phaidon edition the blessed banner presented to William of Normandy by Alexander II is portrayed: in the last example it is held by Eustace, count of Boulogne, who is pointing to William at a vital stage of the battle. The gonfalon is white with a yellow cross between four blue discs; of the three tails one is yellow between two of sanguine. Alexander gave another banner

Pl.XI Two miniatures by Nicholas Hilliard
(1547–1619) showing possibly heraldic symbols.

Pl. XII Left-hand front panel of a *cassone*
(wedding chest) of Guidobaldo Duke of Urbino
(1472–1508) and Elisabetta Gonzaga (*d.*1520)
decorated with a quartered *impresa*:
1] *or, a lamp sable;*
2] *argent, 5 piles wavy issuant from the base gules;*
3] *sable, a chief papelloné per fesse argent and gules;*
4] *or, a capital A in bend sable.*

Fig.48 Duke William's blessed banner held by
Eustace, count of Boulogne. *Courtesy of Phaidon
Press*

and his blessing to Roger Count of Sicily, who was fighting against the
Saracens, and a third, which was said to be 'white with a red cross' to the
reforming party in Milan, led by Herembald – the arms of that city are still
argent, a cross gules.

The Emperor Conrad III, when on crusade in 1146–7, had 'a red banner
with a cross'; and in 1316 the town of Viterbo was granted a banner *gules, a
cross between four keys, wards uppermost, argent,* by the Rector of the Patrimony
of St. Peter, Bernardo Cucuico. In the later part of the fourteenth century
there are examples of the arms of the Church being *gules, a cross between four
pairs of keys in saltire, the wards downwards and tied, argent,* and these colours
continue into the fifteenth century.

The Emperor Frederick I is portrayed as a Crusader in the contemporary
Gesta Frederici I in Italia (*c.* 1190) bearing 'a white shield with a gold cross',
and it was these tinctures, rather than the red and silver, that were adopted
by the Kings of Jerusalem, whose arms appear in the thirteenth century.

Papal heraldry has had an influence outside the Italian peninsula,
particularly on the shape of the vehicle for ecclesiastical arms. These were
not normally displayed upon shields of warlike shape, but on what is known
as a horse's-head or chamfron escutcheon, or upon a circular or oval
cartouche. The emphasis too was not so much upon the shield itself as upon
the insignia of ecclesiastical rank that surround it. Since the Council of
Lyons (1245), there has been some sort of regulated formula for the display
of ecclesiastical arms, but these still reflect the 'Investiture Struggles' which
racked twelfth-century Christendom. Many bishops and abbots, particularly
in the new lands of East and North Germany, were margraves (Eng.
marquesses, rulers of the marches) and consequently combined spiritual and

Fig.49 Standing dish with quarterly arms:
1 & 4: Fugger, *per pale or and azure, 2 fleurs-de-lys counterchanged;*
2: Kirchberg, *argent, a Moorish woman vested sable, crowned or and holding a mitre gules;*
3: Weissenhorn, *gules, 3 horns argent.*
Crests: 1: *a fleur-de-lys per pale azure and or between 2 buffel horns counterchanged;* 2: *the Moorish woman wearing the mitre* (a most unusual crest).

temporal authority in these areas and insignia in their arms. This explains the presence of swords as well as pastoral staves, crooks, and crosses behind such arms.

The Gallican church took over the administrative dioceses of the Roman Empire and many of the duties of the Imperial representative; such magnates as *l'evesq. de beauvais: cōte – or, a cross between four keys gules* – and *l'evesque de laon duc – azure fleuretty or, on a cross argent a crozier in pale gules* – are portrayed among the Knights of the Golden Fleece in the fifteenth-century manuscript 4790 of the Bibliothèque de l'Arsénal[30] as fully armed warriors, with their mitres held near to their banners by angels. In the Provençal *Chanson de geste Ronsavals* (perhaps late twelfth century), the battling archbishop of Reims, Turpin, bears.

> davant si l'escut de son senhal,
> Lo camp fon d'aur e.l cap vermelh e blans

> before him the shield that makes him known,
> A red and white chief, with a field of gold;

and in the *Destruction of Rome* (not before 1200 in its original form) the Pope rides to battle against the Saracens with St.Peter painted on his gonfalon.

Mr Woodward, in his *Ecclesiastical Heraldry*, explains the intricacies of usage at greater length; some clerics who are scions of noble families, it will be noted, wish to draw attention to their position 'in the world', by continuing to use crests, mottoes, supporters (e.g., Nathaniel, Lord Crewe, Prince-Bishop Palatine of Durham, d. 1721); others, more conformably with their Master's teaching, do not (e.g., Dom Peter Gilbey, O.S.B., 9th Lord Vaux of Harrowden, d. 1977).

In England, since the Reformation, all ecclesiastical heraldry has come under the jurisdiction of the College of Arms. A modern Anglican bishop impales his arms with those of his see, the composite shield being surmounted by a mitre; his personal arms, crest and motto – with his wife's arms impaled – appear on another shield *accolé* to the sinister. His Catholic counterpart's arms, however, have no legal standing in this country, for they are granted by a foreign power, the Vatican.

The decline of functional Heraldry

Luca della Robbia's *stemma* of King René, made some time between 1466 and 1478,[31] for Jacopo de'Pazzi's villa at Montughi outside Florence, marks a watershed in heraldic design.

101

The shield, helm, crest and mantling make political statements: those of
the shield we have already discussed; the golden helm affronté affirms
René's kingly status, the mantling and the crest proclaim that he is a cadet of
the French royal house; and the dragons' wings which protect the lily of
France are in the colours of Aragon, to which kingdom he was a serious
pretender.

The crescent with its motto *LOS: EN: CROISSANT* (fame increasing)
stands for the chivalric order that René hoped to initiate. In the fourteenth
and fifteenth centuries large numbers of these were founded (some merely in
imagination, some in real life), but few survived: the Most Noble Order of
the Garter (1348), the Danish Elefantenorden (1462), the Spanish Orders of
Calatrava (1164) and Santiago (1175), and the Orden Militar de Aviz

(1162) in Portugal are among those which have, though not quite in the form originally intended. The more serious had aspirations towards the purification of chivalry, the rescue of the Holy Sepulchre, and the moral betterment of all belonging to them, such as the highly idealistic Order of the Passion (*Militia Passionis Jhesu Christi*) which demanded of the knights a modified version of the three monastic vows (conjugal fidelity replacing celibacy). In this order the knights, according to their rank, were to be dressed in red, green, scarlet and azure with red crosses and hoods of the same colour, and the grand master in white. But many were, as Professor Huizinga shows in *The Waning of the Middle Ages*, a reversion to the 'primitive conception of a club, a game, an aristocratic federation'. Like John the Good's Order of the Star, Louis d'Orléans' Order of the Porcupine, even to some extent the great Burgundian Order of the Golden Fleece, King René's Order of the Crescent would have been a matter of wearing fantastic badges and liveries, affirming one's allegiance to the founder and opposition to his enemies, and taking part in tournaments that in magnificence approximated more and more to the later intricacies of the masque. The Templars, the Hospitallers, the Spanish Order of the Sword (*RUBET ENSIS SANGUINE ARABUM*), had been founded for the defence of Christendom in Outremer or the Iberian Peninsula, where it was most threatened, naturally, but these new elaborations served purely for the glory of man (of one man or family), and are better seen as predecessors of the fashion for personal emblems (and secret meanings – see *imprese*, below) which reached in the sixteenth and seventeenth centuries such heights of beauty and subtlety, and eventually of absurdity.

The decorative border of fruit, as Mr Evans interprets it, alludes to the theme of Virtue and its rewards of Resurrection, Salvation and ultimate Immortality in Christ. The Order of the Crescent and the *DARDANT DESIR* for immortality are two expressions of the same ideal, depicted in mediaeval and in Renaissance terms.

The flames (and indeed the surname) of Pazzi refer to one of Jacopo's ancestors, who, it is said, lit a taper from the Holy Fire at Jerusalem when there on crusade or pilgrimage, and then walked and rode backwards all the way to Florence, shielding the flame, and by some being called mad (*pazzo*).

A story told by Paulus Jovius in his *Dialogo dell'Imprese militari et amorose* shows René and his 'burning zeal' quite differently: 'This is an anecdote that is known to very few, even of those who wear the Tinderbox about their necks and have attached to it the Golden Fleece. The valiant Duke of Burgundy [Charles le Téméraire, 1433–77] used to bear the *Flintstone with the steel and box, and two bundles of wood nearby* to show that he was capable of kindling the fires of war – which he did. However, this valorous man came to a sorry end, for, interfering in the war against Lorraine and the Swiss, he was defeated and killed outside Nancy on the eve of the feast of the Epiphany.

'His *impresa* was mocked by Renato [René, Duke of Lorraine], who said, "Truly this unfortunate man, when he had need to warm himself, had no time to use his tinderbox."

'This saying was the more pithy for on the day of the battle the ground was covered with snow and dyed with blood . . . the greatest cold that had happened in man's memory.'

The change from functional shield and military badge to ornamental escutcheon and personal emblem or *impresa* took place gradually during the end of the fifteenth and beginning of the sixteenth centuries – at different times in different areas. Paulus Jovius wrote: 'But now in our own time, after the coming of Charles VIII [re.1483–98] and Louis XII [1498–1515] into Italy, everyone who followed the profession of arms, imitating the French captains, sought to adorn himself with goodly and pompous *imprese*.' An opposite view is that 'such conceits however were at the beginning of the sixteenth century more characteristic of Italy than of France . . . such badges were introduced to the French by the campaigns in Italy.'[32]

Like the question of the Islamic fleur-de-lys, it is difficult to be sure of the exact place and time of the origin of *imprese*. What is certain is that with the advent of 'modern' weapons and the extinction of the knight as an effective fighting force, the nobility turned more and more towards the decorative and symbolical aspects of heraldry.

True heraldry and *imprese* are often associated, and developments occurred at different times in different countries. The destruction of hundreds of the French chivalry by the English longbow at Agincourt in 1415 should have meant a complete change of tactics, but in the Ashmolean picture of the battle of Pavia we can still see, a little over a century later, a multitude of iron-clad French dinosaurs lumbering blindly through the carnage wrought by crossbows and firearms.

It was the total unwillingness of the mamluks to depart from the ways of *furusiyya* that caused their destruction by the Ottomans, within a few years of Pavia (see p.82). In the West, chivalry and firearms were able to live uneasily together; in the Ottoman Empire there was no knightly class.

According to William Camden's *Remaines of a Greater Worke* (1603), the earliest *impresa* used in England was that of Henry VIII, who at an interview with King François I (the Field of the Cloth of Gold) used for his device *an English archer in a green coat drawing his arrow to the head*, with the motto *CUI ADHAERO PRAEEST* (he whom I join is the winner).

Pl. XIII Dish with the slightly unauthentic impaled arms of Cardinal Antonio di San Severini: *or, 2 pales gules* (San Severino of Venice) and *argent, a fesse and a bordure gules* (San Severino of Verona).

Pl. XIV Dish of the second quarter of the 16th century. Foscarini: *argent, a fesse dancetty azure,* impaling Barberini: *azure, 3 bees or.* It was to

Taddeo Barberini, nephew of Pope Urban VIII (1623-44), that Petra Sancta dedicated his book on Heraldry. The original arms of the Tafani da Barberino were *gules, 3 tafani (horse-flies) or.*

Pl. XV Arms of the Catalonian family of Cabrera. Copper lustre and blue Manises ware of the first half of the 15th century.

IVLII
CAMPI
OPVS
MDXXX

Pl. XVII Tinderbox and flame badge of the Dukes of Burgundy associated with their Order of the Golden Fleece. One of its pursuivants was called *Flint*. The motto *NUL NE SI FROTE* (no-one rubs against me) is a challenge to other factions in French politics and resembles the Scottish *NEMO ME IMPUNE LACESSIT* (no-one touches me with impunity). *Courtesy of the Bodleian Library.*

Pl. XVIII The Villani tournament shield or *pavoise: or, a griffin sable, over all a label of 5 points gules.* A fine piece of heraldic design, but impractical for defensive purposes.

Pl. XVI (On the preceding page) The marriage of Francesco Sforza and Bianca Visconti. He wears a tabard quarterly of his arms and his *impresa. Courtesy of the Bodleian Library*

How then does an *impresa* differ from a badge? The latter is a piece of real heraldry – like the full coat-of-arms, it identifies a particular member of a family and his possessions. An *impresa* serves rather to confuse than to identify: Geoffrey Whitney in his *Choice of Emblems* (1586) explained: '. . . such figures as are wrought in plate or in stones in the pavement or walls for adorning the place: having some wittie device compressed with cunning workmanship, something obscure to be perceived at first, when with further consideration it is understood, it may delight the beholder.' Jovius wrote: 'It should not be so obscure that it needs a Sybil to interpret it, nor so apparent that every rustick may understand it.' Was the significance of the Hillyard miniature of the man clasping a hand from a cloud apparent in 1588 to all but rustics, or was it known only to a few?

Jovius in his *Dialogue* discusses the influence of classical literature and seals upon contemporary *imprese*: 'Vespasian,' he says, used *'a dolphin entangled with an Anchore*, with this Posie: *FESTINA LENTE* [make haste slowly], a sentence that Octavianus Augustus was wont often to use . . . of the famous Palladines of France . . . every one had his peculiar *impresa* or *enseigne*.'

The mid-thirteenth-century *Otinel* bears this out, for in lines 300ff. Roland arms himself thus:

> Au col li pendent .i. fort escu pesant,
> Paint a azur et a or gentement:
> (Envirun l'urle current li quatre vent,
> Li duze signe e li meis ensement,
> Et de l'abisme i est le fundement,)
> Et ciel et terre feit par compassement;
> Dessus la boucle le soleil qui replent . . .

> About his neck a sturdy shield they hung,
> In gold and azure finely done;
> The four winds round the border run,
> The twelve signs and the months each one,
> The pit that lies below, called Baratun,
> Heaven and earth drawn all in one;
> Raised in the middle was the shining sun . . .

This description reminds modern readers of the shield Thetis had made for her beloved son Achilles (*Iliad*, book xviii), which 'consisted of five layers, and Hephaistos decorated it with a number of designs; first of all Earth, Sky and Sea; the unwearied Sun, the Moon at full and all the constellations with which the Heavens are crowned; the Pleiads, the Hyads, great Orion and the Bear, the only constellation that never bathes in Ocean Stream, but always wheels about in the same place and looks across at Orion the Hunter with a wary eye.' Yet the author of *Otinel* could not possibly have been aware of the Greek, though he might have read *Aeneid* viii, the French *Eneas*, or some apocryphon such as Dares' or Dictys' 'history'. Both shields are masterpieces of the whitesmith's art, yet Roland's pride and the arrogance of Achilles led to the deaths of Oliver and Patroclos, and of countless unnamed warriors.

The bright static images of *imprese* often conceal undercurrents which are not always beneficial to the bearer of the shield or his intimates.

When the Swiss were defeated near Milan, at Marignano on 13–14 September 1515, by François I, 'Monsieur de St. Valier (the old man) father of the Ladie Diane de Poictiers, Duchess of Valentinois, & Captain of a hundred gentlemen, bore a standard whereon was pictured *a burning Torch turned upside down, the waxe melting and quenching the same*, with the word: *QUI ME ALIT, ME EXTINGUIT*, being the devise of the King his master, that is: *NUTRISCO ET EXTINGUO* . . . which devise he feigned for love of a lady, wishing to show that as her beauty nourished his thought, so also it put him in danger of his life.'[33]

The device of the *burning torch* to portray the lover destroyed by his love is widely used in *impresa* literature. It seems to imply acceptance, by those adopting it, of the fact that often the aspirations publicised in an *impresa* might well betray their owner: as in the Hillyard *man against a background of flames* (Plate XV):

> Nutrisce il fuoco a lui la cera intorno
> Et la cera l'estingue, o quanti sono
> Che dopo un ricevoto & largo dono
> Dal donator danno a scorno.[34]

> Even as waxe doth feed and quenche the flame,
> So, love gives life: and love, despair doth give:
> The godlie love, doth lovers crown with fame:
> The wicked love, in shame doth make them live.
> Then leave to love, or love as reason will,
> For, lovers lewde doe vainlie languishe still.

Whitney's lines use it to point a moral in the same way as does '*NUTRISCO ET EXTINGUO* with *the Salamander lying in the fire*, which was the badge or Cognizance of François I . . . which worme (Plinie writeth) is of such cold nature that she quencheth the fire like ice. Others write that she liveth, & is

106

norished in the fire. I remember I my self have seene . . . an effigie of a firie Salamander with this inscription, *NUTRISCO IL BUONO & SPENGO IL REO*, that is, I norish the vertuous, and destroy the wicked.'[35]

Imprese and the tournament

By the second half of the sixteenth century the tournament had become a matter of lavish display rather than of brave deeds – once more a vehicle for conspicuous waste against which the Church had preached for so long. The description of two of the knights at an imaginary joust in Italy, from Thomas Nashe's *The Unfortunate Traveller* (1594), is not just a literary fancy:

'The fift[h] was the forsaken knight, whose helmet was crowned with nothing but cipresse and willow garlandes, over his armour he had *Himens* nuptiall robe died in a duskie yelowe, and all to be defaced and discoloured with spots and staines. The enigma, *Nos quoque florimus*, as who should say, we have bin in fashion, his sted was adorned with orenge tawnie eies, such as those have that have the yellow jandies, that make all things yellow they looke uppon, with this briefe, *Qui invident egent*, those that envy are hungry. The sixt was the knight of the storms, whose helmet was rounde moulded lyke the moone, and all his armor like waves, whereon the shine of the moone slightly silverd, perfectly represented moone-shine in the water, his bases were the bankes or shores that bounded in the streames. The spoke was this, *Frustra pius*, as much to saye as fruitlesse service. On his shield hee set foorth a lion driven from his praie by a dunghill cock. The word, *Non vi sed voce*, not by violence but by voyce.'

In 'The most noble and rich tournament made in the magnificent city of Piacenza for the arrival of the most serene Don John of Austria' in 1574, described by Antonio Bendinelli, il Signor Francesco Borgo Colombi appeared as *il cavaliere intento*: he was enclosed in a tower which apparently moved by magic, and preceded by two musicians, a lady dressed in white and silver and gold *all'antica*, two wodwoses, and a wizard all in black with a staff and book. The tower began to emit smoke, fire, and rays as it went along, *con bellissima vista*; and at the end of the stage the lady asked the wizard to free her knight; the wizard complied, and at once the tower exploded (*andò in molti pezzi*), the pieces being carried off by four demons. The knight leaped forth, dressed in the same colours as the lady, of silk and cloth-of-gold, bearing on his shield a crane flying above the clouds, and a fair fruit-tree in a meadow below. His motto was *MAIUS OPUS*. 'Quella

inventione fu riputata da huomini di bellissimo giuditio una delle belle, & sottili, che comparissero à quel Torneo.'

It was followed by three knights, the *Cavalieri Fedeli*, il Signor Conte Francesco Scotti, il Signor Francesco Fogliani, and il Signor Annibale Mancascivolo, all three in the woeful state of having lost their ladies' graces through malicious tongues. They followed a pageant of elegant architectural design, covered in swags, trophies, and paintings, all in silver and gold; Discord sat triumphant on its top; in the middle was Cupid bound; on the left, Jealousy with a long snake wrapped round her; on the right, Disdain, a cheery youth in red and gold. Lamentation followed, in black, with chained feet, and Anxiety, lugubriously dressed, barefoot and dishevelled. The cart was drawn by Harpies (horses quaintly disguised), and the driver was Desire. The knights bore each a shield showing a bush, with on one branch Love's bow and arrows suspended, broken and tied together in a bundle, and the motto *NIL IUVAT*; they were accompanied by musicians and pages, and carried a set of verses each (presumably on a placard).

George Peele's *Polyhimnia* is a verse pamphlet recording what took place 'on 17 November 1590, when Sir Henry Lea, the Queen's Champion, being then fifty-seven, handed over his office to the Earl of Cumberland, and this provided the opportunity for a splendid pageant and display of tilting by chosen pairs of lords and gentlemen of the court'; in it appeared

> all in sables sad/drawne on with coleblacke steedes of duskie hue
> in stately charyot full of deepe device
> Where gloomie tyme sat whippinge on the teame
> iust back to back with this great champyon
> younge Essex: that thrice honorable Earle
> yclad in mighty armes of moorners die
> and plumes as blacke as is the ravens winge

– in mourning for his friend and kinsman Sir Philip Sidney. This array and others like it should be borne in mind by the reader of the allegorical (and apparently imagined) masques and shows in contemporary literature, such as *The Faerie Queene* and the *Arcadia*. Another jouster in this Accession Day Tilt,

> The Earl of Darbies valiant sonne and heire
> brave Ferdinande lord Straunge straungelie embarkt
> under Joves kinglie byrd the golden Eagle
> Stanleyes olde Crest and honourable badge . . .
> vailing his Eagle to his Soveraignes eyes
> as who should say stoope Eagle to this Sun.

Here we see the eagle, which is the crest of Stanley, worked into an almost idolatrous dedication to the Queen, who is portrayed as so powerful that even this King of birds (who according to mediaeval Bestiaries tests the legitimacy of his offspring by making them gaze directly into the sun) must abase his eyes. The crest is used as an *impresa* and as a courtly compliment, perhaps for this one occasion only.

This was not always the case, however: evidence for the permanence of some *imprese* is provided by an illustration (in Litta's *Celebri Famiglie Italiane*) taken from 'un quadro di Giulio Campi nella chiesa di Sancto Sigismundo', of the marriage of Bianca Visconti and Francesco Sforza in 1441. The bridegroom is wearing a surcoat quartered of *undy azure and argent* and *gules, on a mount an apple tree, to which is tethered a hound, issuant from the sinister chief a hand all proper.* This seems to be a very unusual case, where an *impresa* is incorporated in an armorial object, for under the heading *QUIETUM NEMO ME IMPUNE LACESSIT* (in the *Tetrastichi Morali*), the same illustration is assigned to Francesco Sforza, Duke of Milan, with the following quatrain:

> Al pacifico can non date impaccio,
> Diceva Sforza & se qualch'uno il tocca,
> Non si lamente poi della sua bocca
> Sentendo lacerarse il collo o'l braccio.

> 'Let the sleeping dog lie,'
> Said Sforza; if you touch him
> He will tear you arm from limb
> . . . too late then to cry.

It must not be thought, however, that all *imprese* were to be taken completely seriously: Jovius in his *Dialogue* gives instances of unworthy and frivolous conceits such as that of Agustino Porco who, when he was infatuated with Bianca Paltiniera, wore in his crimson cap a white candle, i.e., *CAN DE LA BIANCA* (Bianca's dog), and of Diego de Guzman who, spurned by his lover, wore a bunch of green mallows, i.e., *MAL VA* (it goes badly).

But by 1613 in England a sad decay had set in: Sir Henry Wotton, writing to Sir Edmund Bacon about the Accession Day tilt of that year, tells how

> 'The day fell out wet to the disgrace of many fine plumes. . . Some caparisons seen before adventured to appear again on the stage with a little disguisement . . . so frugal are the times, or so indigent. The

two Riches only made a speech to the King; the rest were contented with bare *imprese*, whereof some were so dark, that their meaning is not yet understood, unless perchance that were their meaning, not to be understood.'

At this tournament, William Shakespeare had designed Lord Rutland's *impresa*, but, infuriatingly, we have no idea of what it consisted; perhaps it was like one of those he had included in *Pericles Prince of Tyre* a few years earlier.

The seventeenth and eighteenth centuries, whether at court or in the country, had not the right climate for heraldry or for *imprese*. The latter become the more and more charged figures of allegory in masques of increasing richness and superficiality, and soon disappear; the art of the former becomes stylised, over-complicated and repetitive.

As early as 1599, Ben Jonson in *Every Man Out of His Humour* was making fun of the new gentlemen:

> '*Sogliardo (reads)*: Gyrony of eight pieces; azure and gules; between three plates, a chevron engrailed checquy, or, vert, and ermins; on a chief argent, between two ann'lets sable, a boar's head, proper.
> *Carlo*: How's that! on a chief argent?
> *Sogliardo (reads)*: On a chief argent, a boar's head proper, between two ann'lets sable.
> *Carlo*: 'Slud, it's a hog's cheek and puddings in a pewter field . . .
> *Sogliardo*: . . . how like you the crest, sir?
> *Puntarvolo*: I understand it not well, what is't?
> *Sogliardo*: Marry, sir, it is your boar without a head, rampant. A boar without a head, that's very rare!
> *Carlo*: Ay, and rampant too! troth, I commend the herald's wit, he has decyphered him well: a swine without a head, without brain, wit, anything indeed, ramping to gentility.'

The Heralds' visitations

Whether or not Sogliardo is typical of the period, it is certainly true that the Tudors organised with great thoroughness, through the College of Arms, the ennoblement of many new men, Welsh *protégés* such as Hugh Vaughan who were granted arms and rank equivalent to the English squires'; and Henry VII at the very end of the fifteenth century had required the Kings of Arms to check and reform if necessary the lists of armigerous gentlemen.

In 1530 Henry VIII conferred letters patent on the College, and these inaugurated the series of Visitations by the Heralds which took place during the next 150 years. The ideal was that each county should be visited every forty years or so and that all false armory should be reformed or defaced.

The results of these Visitations are kept at the College of Arms and have been partly published by the Harleian Society. They are an invaluable aid to genealogy and local history, but the heraldry is often complicated by numerous quarterings and is not always accurate.

The arms of Barrett 'de Titherton Lucas in Com. Wilts.' are given as *or, on a chevron gules between three mullets sable, as many lions passant guardant argent* in 1565, but the field is *argent* in 1623. The Buccleuch hatchment (Plate IV) provides an example of a common abuse: the inescutcheon *argent, three lozenges conjoined in fesse gules, a bordure sable,* quartering *or, an eagle displayed vert, beaked and membered gules,* would lead one to suppose that Elizabeth Montagu was descended from the old baronial families of Montagu and Monthermer. This was not so: her furthest ancestor appears to be a certain William Ladde of Hanging Houghton, in Lamport, co. Northampton (viv.1447), grandfather of Thomas Montagu of Hemington in the same county (viv.1500), whose son Sir Edward was a celebrated lawyer connected by his third marriage with the family of St. Thomas More.

The heralds were accused of granting arms to unworthy applicants who could afford the fees, but it is one of the strengths of the English idea of nobility and gentry that it is an elastic institution based largely upon material wealth and therefore open to all successful men.

Daniel Defoe, writing in 1726, comments:

> 'We see the tradesmen of *England,* as they grow wealthy, coming every day to the Heralds' Office, to search for the Coats of Arms of their ancestors, in order to paint them upon their coaches, and engrave them upon their plate, embroider them upon their furniture, or carve them upon the pediments of their new houses; and how often do we see them trace the registers of their families up to the prime nobility, or the most antient gentry of the kingdom.'[36]

From the eighteenth century to modern times

In the eighteenth century, the Middle Ages were either labelled the Dark Ages or completely misrepresented in strange images, and the power of the College of Arms was disastrously weak. Chatterton's forged charters and poems for a long time fooled educated society. The early years of the nineteenth century, however, saw a renewal of interest in things mediaeval; antiquarian studies, including heraldry and genealogy, became popular, and the works of Sir Walter Scott assured for them a wide and romantically uncritical audience. He witnessed and described the Coronation of George IV on 19 July 1821, when Sir Henry Dymoke the 28th of Scrivelsby, first and last Baronet, acted as Champion in place of his father, the Rev. John Dymoke (aged 57); the Champion rode a horse from Astley's Circus.[37] In preparation for the Eglinton Tournament of 1839, the nobles and squires tilted against a small train, and on the day it rained.[38]

Arms, whether granted or assumed, were displayed in increasingly ostentatious style on what are basically trivial objects – snuff-boxes, fire-screens, door handles, and the like. In some cases heraldic charges divorced from the shield are used in *rococo* design which is reminiscent of Italian Renaissance sculpture, the *imprese* and the funerary architecture of the later Tudor period.

The arms, or in most cases the crest, come not to denote ownership but the social class of the owner. An armorial hall chair in which it is impossible to sit is saying: 'You are now entering the house of someone who is armigerous.'

All was not bad though: in the cases of monumental sculpture, the gateways of large houses, the entrances to some Oxford Colleges and to municipal buildings, and in some funerary art, we find good examples. Here, as with hatchments, bookplates, signet rings, and coach panels, the arms or crest still serve their original purpose of identification, but there is often little life and even less originality. Two of the working drawings from *Heraldic and Ornamental shields for Carriage work* (anon., dated 30 May 1879) illustrate these points: the Grosvenor supporter is not supposed to look like a big pet, but a fierce heraldic hunting hound!

Chinese export porcelain was very popular during the eighteenth century, and it is strange to see how a completely alien group of artists with no knowledge of heraldry tackled the subject. Some, such as the Wills achievement, are very fine; others do not begin to approach Western heraldic criteria, and leave a feeling of intense dissatisfaction. The *three men's heads couped at the neck proper* in the first and fourth quarters of the Fazakerley arms look as though they belonged to criminals executed in Shanghai.

The objects in the Museum do not tell the whole story: during the last decades a great interest in Heraldry has revived in many countries in Europe.

The College of Arms has granted arms to many modern establishments, as well as to towns and individuals: the National Coal Board was granted in 1949 *per fesse argent and sable, three fusils conjoined in fesse counterchanged*, with

Fig.55 Arms of Wills of Saltash, Cornwall, on a
piece of Chinese export porcelain of *c.*1745:
*argent, 3 wyverns passant in pale sable, a bordure
engrailed gules (recte of the 2nd) bezanty.*

British Lions as supporters, appropriately coloured black and charged on the shoulder with a sun to signify heat, light and energy. There is no crest, as a corporation cannot wear one on its helmet, though this is not an invariable rule – e.g., the Atomic Energy Authority (arms granted in 1955) has a crest, of *a sun in splendour* (signifying the peaceful uses of atomic power) *charged with an escutcheon bearing a martlet*, deriving from the arms of Lord Rutherford, the atomic scientist.

There are modern heraldic tiles also in the Museum; for instance the Royal arms, which show how old matter may be artistically treated in a new

Earl Grovesnor

117

Fig.56 Arms of Fazakerley of co.Lancaster on
Chinese export porcelain:
1 & 4: *gules, 3 men's heads couped at the neck proper*
on each a cap argent – Fazakerley;
2: *ermine, 2 bars vert* – Fazakerley;
3: *sable, 3 swans argent* – Fazakerley;
impaling Lutwyche of co.Salop, *or, a tiger*
passant gules.

way without either losing its character or constraining the modern artist to slavish imitation of the ancients.

On 2 March 1984 the College of Arms celebrated its five-hundredth anniversary. This small work is dedicated equally to that august body and to the Victoria and Albert Museum. May the College continue to be the instigator of fine heraldic work, and the corrector of the bad and indifferent, and may the Museum continue to collect examples of the former and shun the latter.

FOOTNOTES

1. As early as 1382 an anonymous treatise is entitled *De Heraudie*.
2. Sinope, a town in Paphlagonia from which is obtained *sinopis*, 'red earth' in Low Latin.
3. From German *blasen*, to blow a horn. A flourish of trumpets would precede the description of the arms of combatants in a tournament.
4. The mistake derives from the French *barre*, a bend sinister, and *cotice-barre*, a bendlet sinister; see below Plate IV, where a baton sinister is used to denote illegitimate descent from Charles II.
5. Here both the billets and the lion are gold; therefore it is not necessary to define their tincture twice.
6. See Sir Frank Stenton and Professor Francis Wormald, in their respective chapters on 'The Historical Background' and 'Style and Design' of *The Bayeux Tapestry* (Phaidon, 1965).
7. In the *Chanson d'Aspremont* (perhaps written *c.*1188) the French preparing to fight a huge army of Saracens 'De roges crois se vont trestot croissant; Per ce ira l'uns l'altre conissant' (lines 4408f.). They cross themselves with red crosses, so that one will know another.
8. See glossary.
9. Léon Gautier, *La Chevalerie* (1884).
10. The use of *celestre* (*bleu céleste*) is unusual, particularly as a synonym for *bis*, which is much darker, duller colour, but obviously the author must have an assonance for St. Denis!
11. Miss Harvey in *Moriz von Craûn and the Chivalric World* (O.U.P. 1961) gives a valuable account of the social and literary background which emphasises the ambivalence of the tournament as a whole.
12. *Traittié de la forme et devis comme on fait les tournois*, of 1460–65 (Ms. fr. 2695 in the Bibliothèque Nationale).
13. It is current heraldic practice to define a shield as quarterly of so many pieces, rather than saying fifthly, sixthly, etc.
14. British Library MS. Egerton 1070, fol.4v.
15. G. Brault in *Early Blazon* quotes Littré's *Dictionnaire* (1875–7): 'fleur imaginaire à feuilles arrondies, tantôt au nombre de cinq . . . tantôt de six.'
16. British Library MS. Royal 14 C VII.
17. Translated by P. Hitti as *An Arab-Syrian gentleman* (Columbia U.P., 1929).
18. Leaf, *Journal of the Royal Asiatic Society* (1983/II)
19. *Ibid.*
20. Quoted by L.A.Mayer in his fundamental work *Saracenic Heraldry* (O.U.P. 1933).
21. MS Hazine 841 from the Topkapi Museum, Istanbul, of the first quarter of the thirteenth century.
22. Per pale azure and purpure, three lucies' heads erased or, swallowing as many spear-heads argent.
23. Mayer, *op.cit.*
24. Dr Michael Meinecke, *Zur mamlukischen Heraldik* (1973).
25. From the original grant in the Trésor des Chartes, copied by the Abbé Legrand in the eighteenth century.
26. *Life of Saladin* by Behâ ed-Dîn, Palestine Pilgrims Text Society, vol.XIII (1897).
27. Ibn Zunbul, *Fath Misr* 30 and 104
28. It has also been suggested that Henry may have intended to found another Order of Chivalry, of the Holy Spirit, to bolster up his claim to the throne with the suggestion of

divine election, and that the letters stand for SANCTUS SPIRITUS.

29. *Papal Heraldry* (London, 1972), p.61.

30. Published in 1971 by Heraldry Today, as *A European Armorial*, ed. Rosemary Pinches and Anthony Wood.

31. According to Mark Evans of the Walker Art Gallery, Liverpool, who has published the *stemma* in *Victoria and Albert Masterpieces*, sheet 23. If the wings and the escutcheon of pretence of Aragon are meaningful, it must have been made after 1467, but not long after 1470, when René relinquished his claims to that kingdom.

32. Dr Joan Evans, *Pattern in Western Europe* (O.U.P. 1931).

33. *Portratures . . . of Gabriel Simeon* (1562)

34. Claude Paradin, *Symbolica Heroica* (Antwerp, 1567), translated into English by P.S. as *Heroicall Devises* (London, 1591).

35. *Op. cit.*

36. Daniel Defoe, *The Complete English Tradesman*, quoted by Sir Anthony Wagner, *English Genealogy* (O.U.P. 1960).

37. Burke's *Landed Gentry* (1952).

38. Ian Anstruther, *The Knight and the Umbrella* (London, 1963).

FURTHER READING

Throughout this work we have referred, in the text, to a number of books the reader may find helpful or entertaining; some are centuries old, or difficult to get hold of for some other reason. There are probably thousands of books about heraldry (an early nineteenth-century bibliography, Bernd's *Wappenwissenschaft*, runs to two closely-printed volumes), but these few may serve as starting-points:

Vocabulaire-Atlas Héraldique (Société du Grand Armorial de France, Paris, 1952)
Julian Franklyn, *Shield and Crest* (MacGibbon & Kee, 1961).
L.G.Pine, *Heraldry, Ancestry and Titles* (Heinemann 1965).
L.G.Pine, *The Genealogist's Encyclopedia* (David and Charles 1969).
Boutell's Heraldry (revised edition, Warne, 1966).
G.Brault, *Early Blazon* (O.U.P., 1972).
Sir Rodney Dennys, *The Heraldic Imagination* (Barrie & Jenkins, 1975).

GLOSSARY OF HERALDIC AND RELATED TERMS

accollé: related shields side by side, either touching or overlapping slightly.

achievement: the complete armorial bearing

addorsed or **endorsed**: back to back.

alerion: an eagle displayed, shown beakless and legless.

amir: an officer in the Muslim army who may well have administrative power.

arms: the armorial bearings depicted on the shield.

badge: a personal device, in war displayed on standards and used by one's mesnie; in time of peace it identifies one's property, but is used more in Scotland than elsewhere (see below, *crest*)

bar: a narrow horizontal strip; the shield can be *barry* of any even number (but *sable five bars* or *barrulets or*).

barbel: a fish of the pike family; the *canting* (q.v.) charge of the lordship of Bar.

baridi: despatch rider, whose insignia may have been a *fesse* (q.v.)

baston or **baton**: a *bendlet couped*; the *insignia* of office of the Earl Marshal.

bend: a strip running from *sinister* chief to *dexter* base; the diminutive is a *bendlet*, and a shield can be *bendy* (see above, *barry*).

billet: a small rectangle; if the shield is *semy* (q.v.) of billets, it can be called *billetty*.

blazon: the correct armorial description of a shield or *achievement* (see note 3).

bordure: a strip running around the edge of a shield (when the shield is *impaled* [q.v.] however, it does not normally follow the palar line).

bunduqdar: bowman; insignia a bow, or a bow and arrows.

cadency: *differences* (q.v.) for junior members of a family (see the English and Scottish systems on p.34).

canting: *armes parlantes*, where the charges make some reference to the owner's name, e.g., the trellis of Maltravers, which is hard to get through.

canton: a half-quarter in chief.

capo d'Angiò: a chief of allegiance to the Guelf, Papal or Angevin party in the Italian internecine struggles.

capo d'impero: a chief of allegiance to the Ghibelline or Imperial party.

charge: an object portrayed naturalistically or stylised either on the *field* (q.v.) or on another charge.

checky: a field or charge divided into small squares.

chevron: an inverted V; the diminutive is *chevronel*, and a field can be *chevronny*.

chief: the top one-third of the shield, separated horizontally.

coat of arms: see *achievement*.

College of Arms: the corporation of the Kings, Heralds and Pursuivants in Queen Victoria Street, London, of which Garter King of Arms is the President. Under him are two other Kings, Clarenceux, and Norroy and Ulster, who administer the counties South and North of the River Trent respectively. They are assisted by Lancaster, Chester, Windsor, York, Somerset and Richmond, the heralds, and by four pursuivants, Rouge Croix, Rouge Dragon, Portcullis and Bluemantle.

compartment: the solid area on which the *supporters* (q.v.) rest; it can be depicted naturally, as grass or water, or architecturally.

compony: an area divided into rectangles of contrasting tinctures.

couped: cut off as with an axe.

Court of the Lord Lyon: the Scottish equivalent of the College of Arms; the King is the Lord Lyon, who is in charge of three heralds, Marchmont, Rothesay, and Albany, assisted by as many pursuivants, Unicorn, Falkland and Carrick. Unlike the

English officers, who are members of the Royal Household, those in Scotland are civil servants, and the court still has the power to try cases of misuse of arms.

crest: a symbol of recognition, which surmounts the helm and is frequently used to identify one's property. Not all families have crests, and it is totally incorrect to refer to the *achievement* as a 'crest'.

cross, **crosslet**, **cross-crosslet**, **crusilly**: these may be of many forms; if the arms terminate in crosses, it is called a *cross-crosslet*; *crusilly* means *semy* of small crosses.

cuir bouillé: leather softened by boiling and shaped to form protective armour, crests, etc.

dawadar: secretary; insignia, a penbox.

dexter: the right-hand side of the shield as one holds it.

diapered, **diapering**: see p.18

differencing: slightly changing the coat-of-arms to show a family or territorial alliance or other kind of dependence.

dimidiation: a primitive form of *impalement*, which has long been discontinued, though examples still exist.

dragon: an ancient mythological composite beast, traditionally identified with the forces of evil. In the *Chansons de Geste* it is a three-dimensional windsock banner in the shape of this beast, and hence any banner or standard.

eagle: symbol of royalty used by both Christian and Muslim dynasties. They are most often depicted displayed, that is, hovering, with either one or two heads.

Earl Marshal: the visitor and overlord of the College of Arms. The office has been held by successive Dukes of Norfolk since 1677.

enseignes: see *insignia*.

erased: torn off.

escu, **escutcheon**: a pointed shield.

fesse: a horizontal strip of about one-third of the area of the shield; the diminutive is called a *bar* (q.v.).

field: the background of a shield, either plain, divided, or *semy*; it is always blazoned first.

fleur-de-lys: a formalised lily or iris, traditionally associated with the Trinity; it was called 'Frankish' by the Muslims (see p.36) and they may have seen it as referring to the three People of the Book, themselves, the Christians, and the Jews.

foreign Heraldry: see Pine's *Genealogist's Encyclopedia*, which in the chapter on Heraldry gives an extensive list of works on European blazon and related subjects.

fusil: a distaff, depicted as an elongated *lozenge* (q.v.). A field or charge may be *fusilly*.

garnished: decorated, e.g., *a sword arg. garnished or*.

gonfalon: a large banner pendent from a cross-bar.

guardant: looking towards the spectator.

gutty, **goutté**: spotted with drops of liquid

gyron: a triangular half-quarter; an area divided in this way is *gyronny*.

hatchment: a funereal *achievement*, in commemoration (see p.27).

helm, **helmet**: part of the *achievement* which supports the *crest*: the shape and metal differ according to the bearer's rank.

heraldic heiress: the female representative of a family of which there are no surviving males (if there is more than one, they are co-heiresses).

impalement: the arms of two families divided *per pale* on the same shield to show a marital alliance (sometimes arms of office are combined in this way with personal arms to show that a man is 'married' to his job, see p.29).

impresa: see p.103 ff.

inescutcheon of pretence or **in pretence**: a coat-of-arms placed in *fesse point* to show a pretence or claim to additional land or honours.

insignia: distinguishing devices, usually on a shield, which may or may not be heraldic. The Old French *enseignes* can mean arms or insignia.

jamdar: Master of the Robes; insignia, a napkin.

jashnikir: taster; insignia, a tray.

jukandar: polo-master; insignia, polosticks, sometimes with balls.

label: a strip of material with an odd number of pendents; it normally signifies that the bearer is the eldest son of an armiger and is removed when the father dies.

lambrequin: see *mantling*.

lines of division: see p.23.

lion: an obvious symbol of royalty. No Western herald had ever seen a lion, and therefore they are depicted in a stylised manner to denote power and ferocity; if there are more than two on a shield they are called *lioncels* (Old French *lionceaus*).

lozenge: a diamond shape. A field covered in them is *lozengy*.

lucy: the more usual name in heraldry for a pike; the *canting charge* of the Lucy family (see *barbel*).

Lyon Clerk Depute: research assistant to the Lord Lyon; the office was discontinued in 1890.

malik: a Muslim title equivalent to 'prince'.

mamluk: a non-Muslim slave who was educated in the Qu'ran and in arms, and could become an amir (q.v.).

mantling: a short piece of stylised cloth flowing from the *helmet* and behind the shield.

martlet: a legless bird which probably represents a swift.

mascle: the outline of a *lozenge*; a field covered in them is *masculy*.

motto: a memorable word or saying which may form part of the *achievement*; they are entirely personal, and do not form part of the grant of arms.

mullet or **molet**: the stylised form of a spur-rowel, which resembles a five-pointed star.

murex: a shellfish from which purple dye is obtained.

ordinary: an important geometrical charge (see p.18).

orle: a *bordure* (q.v.) separated from the edges of the shield; *charges* can be placed *in orle*.

Outremer: literally, 'overseas'; the Holy Land.

pale: a vertical stripe; its diminutive is a *palet*, and a shield divided into vertical stripes is *paly*.

panache: a bunch of feathers used as, or in place of, a *crest*.

passant: pacing (unless otherwise stated, from *sinister* to *dexter*).

patonce: trifurcated terminals of the arms of a cross.

pommy, pometty: a *cross* whose arms end in *roundles*.

potent: a *cross* whose arms end in T-shapes.

quarter, quartering, quarterly: see p.25.

quarto dell'impero: a quarter of the Empire (see *capo d'impero*).

queue fourchée: with a forked tail.

rampant: pouncing.

reguardant: looking backwards.

rose: a five-petalled wild rose in Western heraldry. In Muslim *insignia*, the rosette was a symbol of royalty and resembles Far Eastern representations.

roundle: see p.34.

saltire: a St. Andrew's cross.

saqi: cup-bearer; insignia, a cup.

satrany: a checker-board banner carried by Muslim armies.

semy: strewn or powdered with small *charges*.

silahdar: armour-bearer; insignia, a sword, dagger, or scimitar.

stains: mixed colours which in origin were probably vegetable dyes (see p.15).

stemma: (Italian, from Latin) a pedigree or a coat-of-arms giving genealogical information.

supporter: a three-dimensional figure which supports the shield in some *achievements* (see p.15).

tamga: an ancient *charge* used in some Muslim *insignia*, which reappears in large numbers in Eastern European arms (see p.76).

targe: a round shield, in the *Chansons de geste* often associated with the Muslim warriors.

tiara: the triple crown of the Papacy.

tinctures: the colours, metals, furs and stains of the heraldic artist.

trapper: protective covering for a war-horse; on it were frequently depicted the arms of the warrior.

tressure: diminutive of the *orle*; a decorated double tressure is frequently found in Scots heraldry.

trianguly: a *field* or *charge* divided into isosceles triangles.

tricking: a method of indicating the colours of a *blason* (see p.18).

vambraced: in full armour (used of the arm).

voided: with the centre part removed.

ward: the working parts of a key.

wreath: material of two or more *tinctures*, twisted about the *helm* where the base of the *crest* is fixed.